MURDER ON THE NIGHT SLEEPER

SLEEPER TRAINS IN POPULAR CULTURE

DAVID MEARA

AMBERLEY

Vicissitudes of travel very strange, and am struck – as often – by enormous dissimilarity between journeys undertaken in real life, and as reported in fiction. Can remember very few novels in which train journey of any kind does not involve either *(a)* Hectic encounter with member of opposite sex, leading to tense emotional issue; *(b)* discovery of murdered body in hideously battered condition, under circumstances which utterly defy detection; *(c)* elopement between two people each of whom is married to somebody else, culminating in severe disillusionment, or lofty renunciation.

Nothing of all this enlivens my own peregrinations, but on the other hand, the night not without incident.

E. M. Delafield, *Diary of a Provincial Lady* (1930)

First published 2026

Amberley Publishing
The Hill, Stroud,
Gloucestershire, GL5 4EP

www.amberley-books.com

ISBN: 978 1 3981 2087 7 (print)
ISBN: 978 1 3981 2088 4 (ebook)

British Library Cataloguing in Publication Data.
A catalogue record for this book is available from the British Library.

Typeset in 10pt on 13pt Celeste.
Typesetting by SJmagic DESIGN SERVICES, India.
Printed in UK.

Appointed GPSR EU Representative: Easy Access System Europe Oü, 16879218
Address: Mustamäe tee 50, 10621, Tallinn, Estonia
Contact Details: gpsr.requests@easproject.com, +358 40 500 3575

Contents

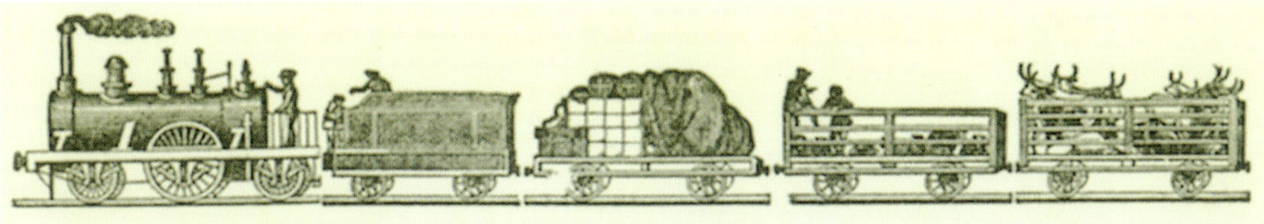

Woodcut of an early steam train.

Acknowledgements

It has been a real pleasure to research and write this book. I have gained much useful material from those who have written about sleeper trains, and the many writers of murder mystery fiction, many of whom are included in the Bibliography. In my researches I would also like to thank the staff at the Science and Society Picture Library, especially Ellie; Wagons-Lits Diffusion, especially Arnaud; the National Portrait Gallery London, especially Bruna; *Life Magazine*, especially Amy; Shutterstock, especially Sam and Belén; Mark Terry at Facsimile Dust Jackets, LLC, San Francisco; Penguin Random House; The Friends of the West Highland Lines, especially Norman McNab for his splendid images; Tracey Salt of TJS Typing Services for typing and retyping my manuscript with great patience; The Oxford Duplicating Centre, especially Ali and Cheryl; Jo Charrington for taking on typing my manuscript at short notice; the team at Amberley Publishing for their help and encouragement; and, as always, my wife Rosemary for her unfailing love, support and interest.

Every effort has been made to seek permission for the use of the images used in this book. If an image has been incorrectly attributed, please contact the publisher, and we will endeavour to make the necessary correction at the earliest opportunity.

Introduction

'All Aboard!'

Two of my lifelong pleasures have been railways and detective fiction. My first memory of the excitement of steam trains dates from 1950 when my grandfather took my brother and me to the railway bridge at Wolvercote over the lines running north from Oxford to watch the expresses gathering speed on their way to Birmingham and the Midlands. I remember vividly the smoke from the steam engines billowing up and over the bridge and enveloping us as we hid inside our grandfather's overcoat. When we travelled to Scotland on family holidays from 1959 onwards we always used the overnight sleeper train from Euston to Inverness, known as the Royal Highlander. The sense of excitement and adventure I felt all

The Caledonian Sleeper near Gorton on the West Highland Line to Fort William, Scotland. In this remote area on the edge of Rannoch Moor there was a signal box and passing place before the wilderness of the moor, which features in Robert Louis Stevenson's novel *Kidnapped.* (Norman McNab)

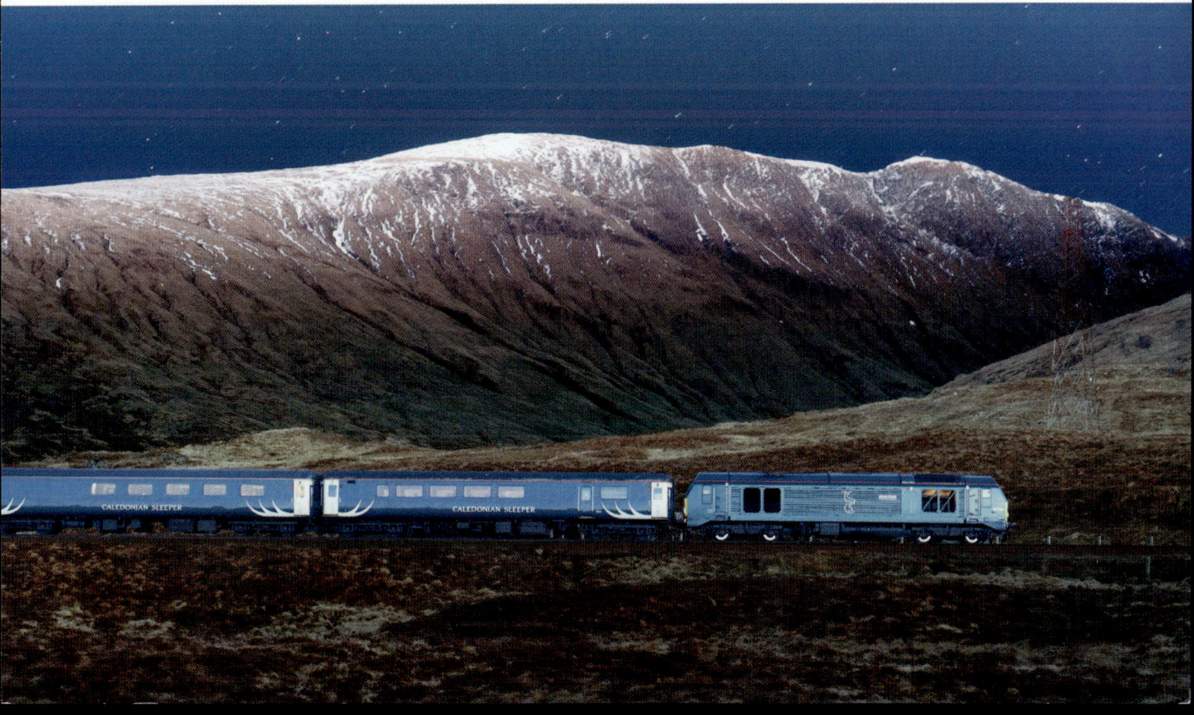

those years ago has never left me, and I have travelled many times on the Scottish sleepers since then. There is something about an overnight train that is both romantic and slightly unnerving; the feeling that on such a long and complex journey things could easily go wrong during the hours of darkness.

My first introduction to detective fiction came when in 1959, aged twelve, I received as a prep school prize the *Selected Stories of Sherlock Holmes* by Sir Arthur Conan Doyle in a nicely bound Oxford edition. If Edgar Allan Poe was the inventor of the detective novel, with his *The Murders in the Rue Morgue* in 1841, then Arthur Conan Doyle really turned it into a popular literary genre, with the forensic and logical detective Sherlock Holmes and his faithful assistant Dr Watson, and his wonderful evocation of the atmosphere of Victorian and Edwardian London. These tales whetted my boyish appetite and I was soon

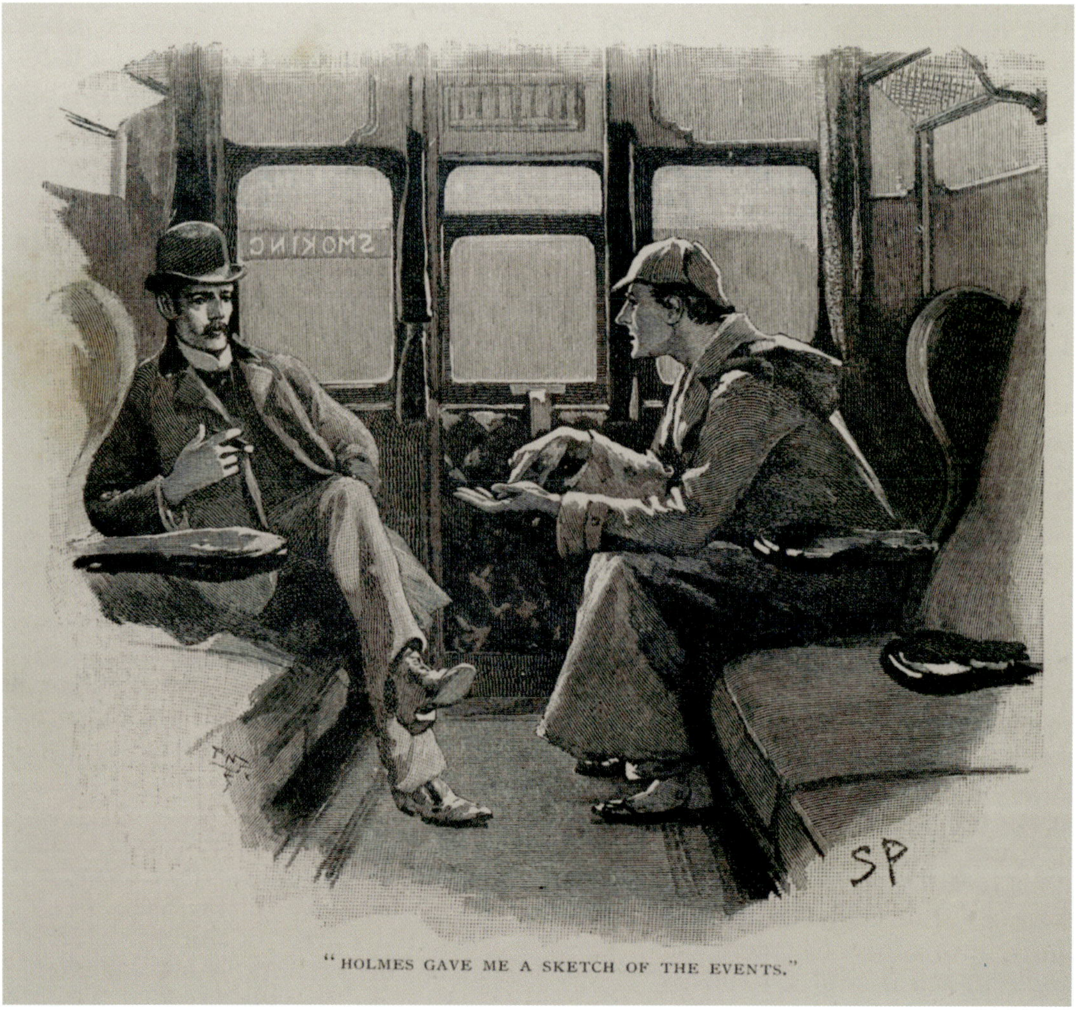

'Holmes gave me a sketch of the events.' Sherlock Holmes and Dr Watson in a first-class compartment on the train from London Paddington to Exeter. From *Silver Blaze*, illustration by Sidney Paget, in the *Strand Magazine*, December 1892.

exploring the extensive canon of detective fiction, especially the writers from what came to be known as the 'Golden Age of Detective Fiction' in the years between the two world wars, Agatha Christie, Dorothy Sayers, Margery Allingham, J. I. M. Stewart, R. Austin Freeman and others. During this period certain conventions were established for the genre: the 'whodunnit' format, a light-hearted straightforward approach and a predilection for upper-class settings such as country houses.

The poet W. H. Auden, for whom detective stories were an addiction, wrote a definitive essay on the underlying principles of the genre in *Harper's Magazine* in 1948, entitled 'The Guilty Vicarage: Notes on the Detective Story by an Addict'. Auden likens the best detective stories to the conventions of Greek tragedy, in which there is Concealment (who is the guilty one?) and Manifestation (the truly guilty person is exposed). He says that the detective story requires both a closed society so that the possibility of an outside murderer is excluded and also a closely related society so that all the members are potential suspects. He points out that these conditions are met when a group of people is isolated in a neutral place, a setting for which an overnight sleeping car train is ideally suited.

Coincidentally the Golden Age of Detective Fiction coincided with the 'Golden Age of the Railways', when the train services in Britain, on the Continent and in America reached heights of luxury never since surpassed. So, it was natural that railway trains should become an ideal setting for a murder/mystery novel or a thriller, and of all the types of train, as W. H. Auden pointed out, the overnight sleeper train affords the most promising setting for murder and mayhem to unfold. The combination of a closed environment on the move, a private sleeping compartment, a smart restaurant car in which suspects can interact with each other and a long journey through the hours of darkness to exotic far-flung locations offers a multitude of opportunities for the unravelling of a story of suspense, romance and mystery.

After the opening of the Stockton & Darlington Railway in 1825 it didn't take long for the rapidly expanding railway system to be woven into contemporary fiction. From the beginning, the iron monster racing through the countryside belching out smoke and steam and frightening the cattle in the fields along the way was seen as an object both of wonder and fear. Charles Dickens was equally fascinated and horrified by the concept of train travel, not surprisingly after being himself involved in a train crash at Staplehurst on 9 June 1865, in which ten people died. In his novel *Dombey and Son*, written between 1846 and 1848 when the railway was revolutionising transport and bringing both social upheaval and greater prosperity, the railway engine becomes a symbol for the inevitable force of mortality: 'The power that forced itself – upon its iron way – its own – defiant of all paths and roads, piercing through the heart of every obstacle, and dragging living creatures of all classes, ages and degrees behind it, was a type of the triumphant monster, Death.' In his stories such as *Mugby Junction* and *The Signalman*, which involve the railway, Charles Dickens made use of the social and psychological aspects of rail travel 'to weave into his narrative the varied and complex responses to the profound changes accompanying that transport revolution. The train brought with it construction, destruction, growth, death, progress, fear. It changed the nature of travel, the way we perceive the world and our notions of place.' John Edmondson, 'Charles Dickens on Railway Development and Rail Travel in *Dombey and Son*', *BackTrack*, November 2017.

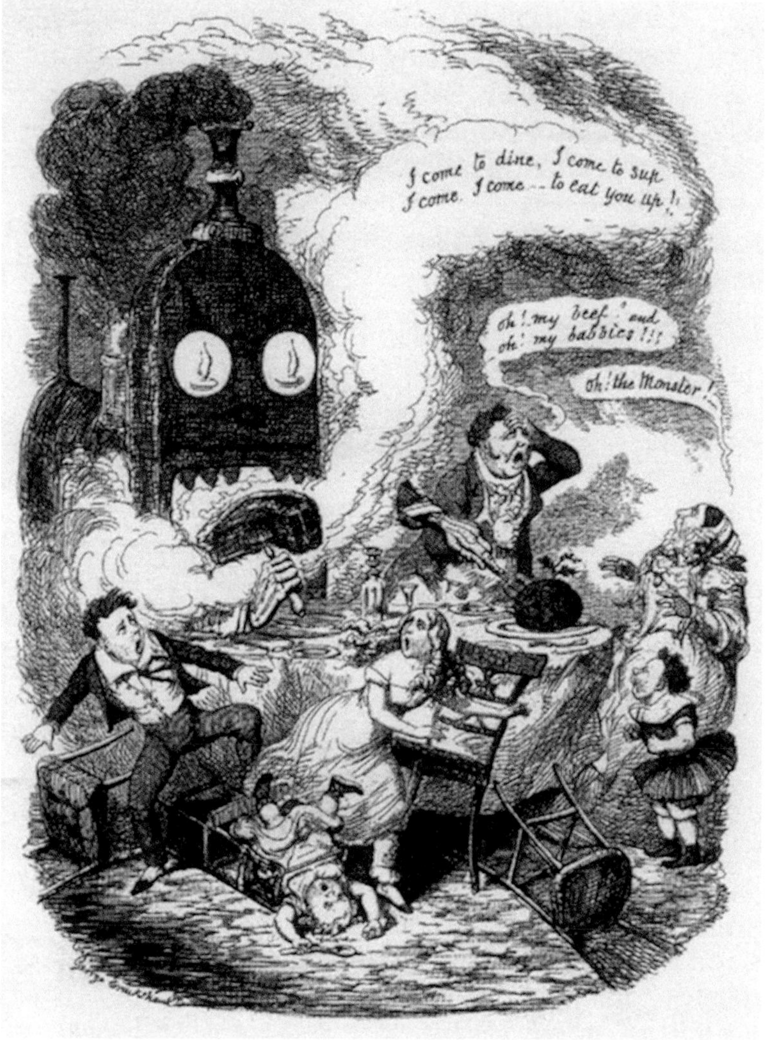

'The Railway Dragon', a cartoon by George Cruickshank, 1845, in *The Table Book.* A terrifying anthropomorphic railway engine crashes into the dining room of a family celebrating Christmas and devours their meal.

The depiction of the engine and its carriages as both an agent of progress and an instrument of death reaches its peak in Émile Zola's novel *La Bête humaine*, published in 1890. The title translates as *The Beast in Man* but metaphorically as *The Human Beast*, which can also refer to the railway engine itself. In this psychological thriller Zola tells a story written within the railway system of the time. Using characters who have appeared in other novels of his – Etienne Lantier, the homicidal and rapacious engine driver, Roubaud, the deputy Station Master at Le Havre, and his wife Séverine – Zola weaves a complex tale of murder, jealousy and marital infidelity which culminates with the outbreak of the Franco-Prussian War in 1870, when a train full of French soldiers heading for the front is left driverless, as Lantier, guilt-ridden over his part in the deaths of Roubaud and Séverine, falls to his death. The express train powers on, 'Bound for the future, heedless of spilt blood.' Here the railway engine is seen as a soul-less mechanical monster, an agent of death.

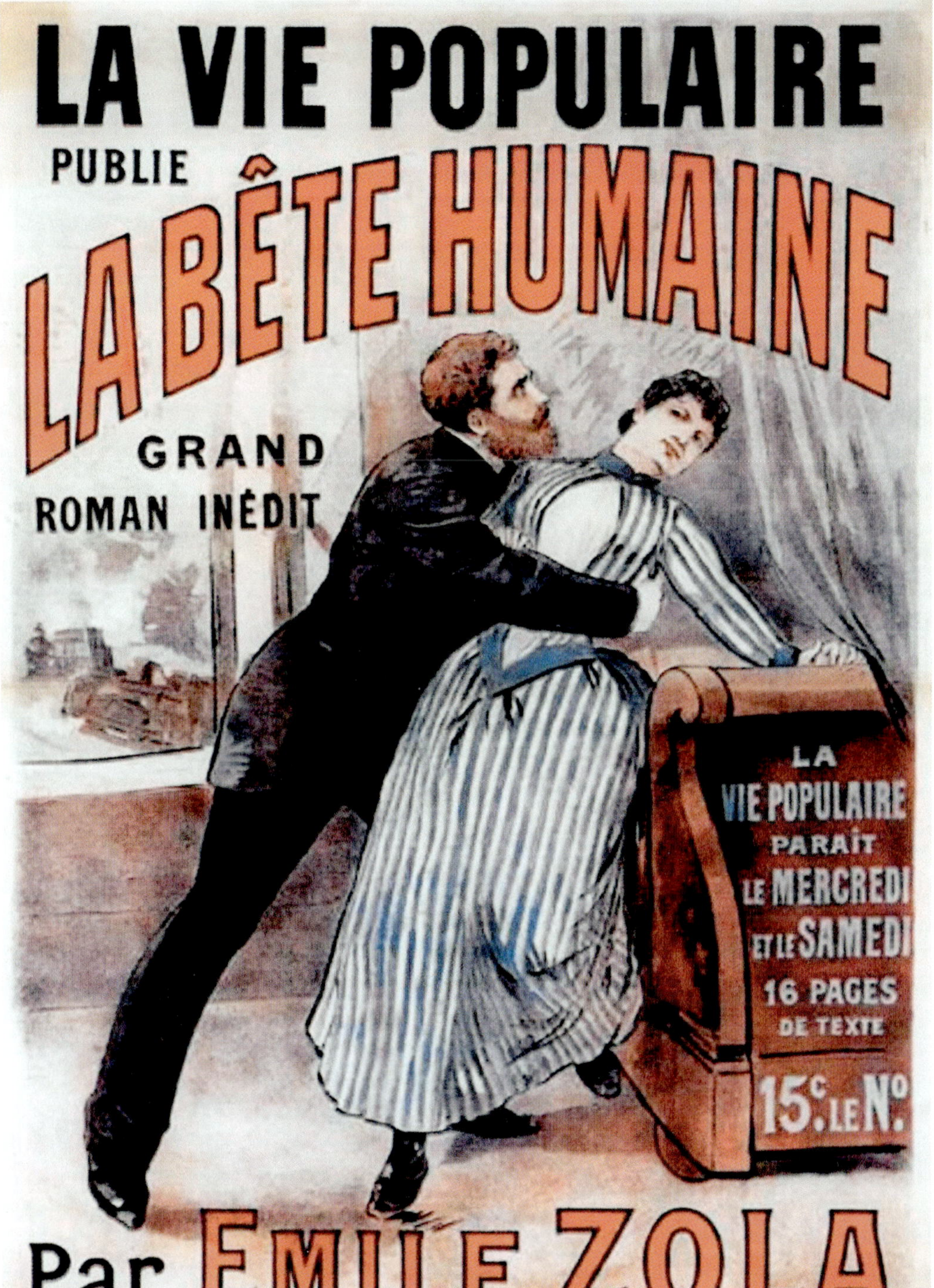

An advertisement for *La Bête humaine* by Emile Zola in *La Vie Populaire,* 1889. (Bibliothèque Nationale de France)

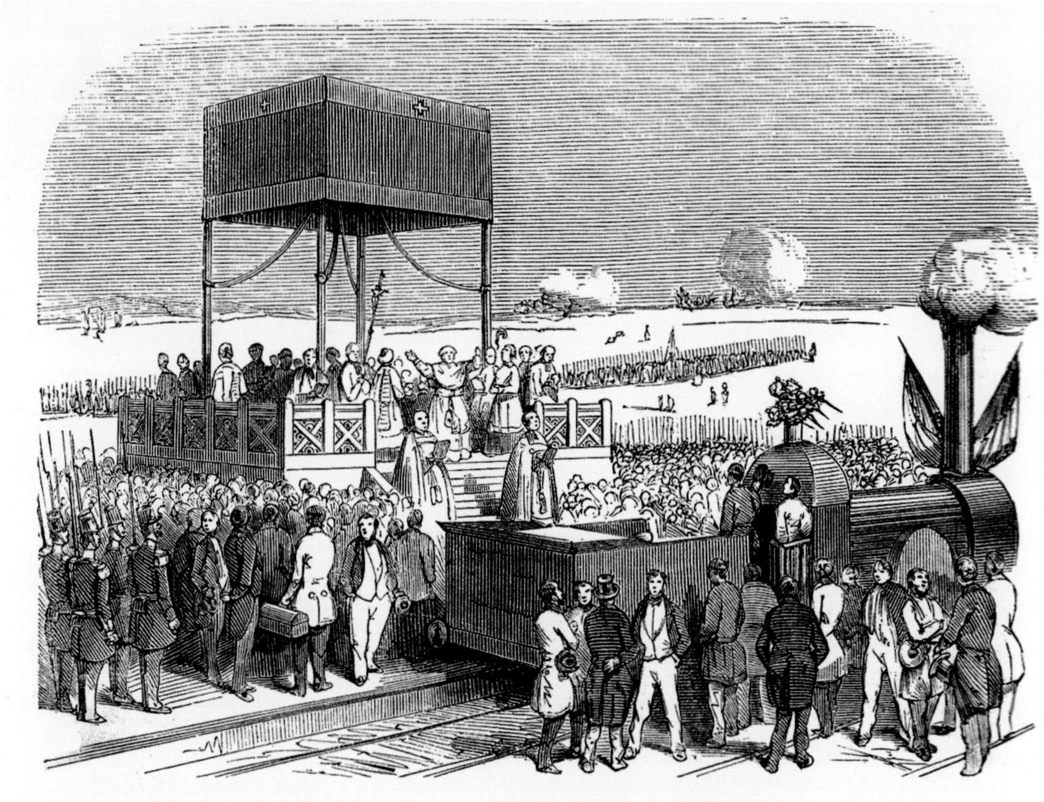

Fêtes de Calais. — Bénédiction du Chemin de fer.

Blessing ceremony for a steam locomotive at Calais in 1848. The image suggests that at the time steam locomotives were seen as fearsome objects that needed the prayers of the church to keep them and the public safe. (Wikipedia Commons)

As the nineteenth century progressed, attitudes towards the railways slowly mellowed, and they came to be accepted as benign agents of progress and simply part of the landscape. Think of *The Railway Children* by E. Nesbit, (1905). Here the railway, its trains and employees are seen as the gentle setting in which the children, whose father has been imprisoned for spying, seek to prove his innocence. The railway symbolises both the idyllic family life that has been broken, and the links that still bind them to the past and give them hope. As Andrew Martin has commented about this change of emphasis: 'The question had become not so much whether the express had managed to reach its destination in one piece as the far more benign: "Was it two minutes late?"' ('On the right track', *The Guardian*, 17 November 2007). So, by the time of the first Sherlock Holmes stories, by Sir Arthur Conan Doyle, serialised in the *Strand Magazine*, beginning with *A Study in Scarlet* (1887) and *The Sign of Four* (1890), the railways were as much a part of the landscape as cars and motorways are today. It has been calculated that a railway journey in the Holmes canon is mentioned in thirty-four out of fifty-six of the short stories and in three of the novels. A typical example is *Silver Blaze* in which Holmes startles Dr Watson by calculating the speed of the Great Western Railway Express in which they are travelling to Tavistock by noting the telegraph posts flashing past. Later, when returning to London, they enjoy the luxury of a Pullman coach on the London & South Western Railway. Nigel Rigby, in an article in *BackTrack* (December 2007, pp. 719–24) gives an exhaustive account of the railway journeys and timings in the canon, showing that Conan Doyle was surprisingly accurate in his depiction of the railways in his Sherlock Holmes stories.

A near contemporary of Conan Doyle (1859–1930) was the clergyman and writer the Revd Canon Victor Alonzo Whitechurch (1868–1933), who had a great interest in railways, and who is best known for his detective stories featuring Thorpe Hazell, a railway detective. During his ecclesiastical career Whitechurch was vicar of Blewbury in Berkshire and later chaplain to the Bishop of Oxford. His short stories were published as *Thrilling Stories of the Railway* in 1912 and include titles such as *The Affair of the Corridor Express, How the Express was Saved* and *The Slip Coach Mystery*. Dorothy Sayers admired him for his immaculate plotting and factual accuracy, and his stories often feature technical details of railway operational practice, including signalling, shunting and intricate timetable plotting, and are set both in Britain and on the Continent.

Whitechurch's eccentric detective Thorpe Hazell is described as 'a slight, delicate-looking man with a pale face and refined features, light red hair and dreamy blue eyes ... a gentleman ... whose knowledge of book editions and bindings was only equalled by his grasp of railway details'. Sadly, Whitechurch only sets one of his stories on what must be a sleeper train to Scotland, as we shall see in Chapter 2. Another near contemporary of Whitechurch was Dr Richard Austin Freeman (1862–1943) who wrote many detective stories and was the first to use the device of opening the story with a depiction of the crime, usually including the identity of the perpetrator, followed by the detective's attempt

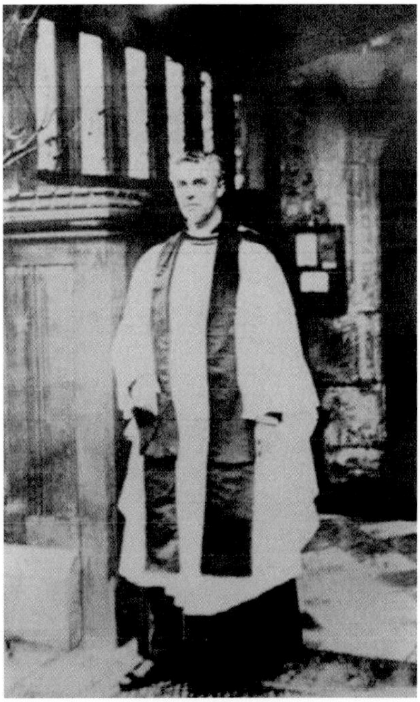

The Revd Canon Victor Alonzo Whitechurch (1868–1933). (Wikipedia Commons)

to solve the mystery. He wove some of his experiences as a surgeon in the Colonial Service into his fiction, and in *Dr John Evelyn Thorndyke* created the archetypal forensic scientific detective. In his 1932 novel *When Rogues Fall Out* the murder of a policeman, Inspector Badger, takes place in Greenhithe Tunnel on the Dartford/Strood line in Kent. Austin Freeman's Dr Thorndyke has often been compared with Sherlock Holmes and is generally regarded as a more accurate thinker and superior scientist, although Conan Doyle's stories undoubtedly have a higher literary merit.

Another more famous contemporary of Austin Freeman is John Buchan, who became the 1st Baron Tweedsmuir (1875–1940). During the First World War he became Director of Information for the British government, and wrote his first thriller spy story *The Thirty-Nine Steps* in 1915, the first of many to feature his hero Richard Hannay. Hannay uses the railway network in Britain extensively, travelling on the 7.10 a.m. train from St Pancras in London to Galloway at the start of *The Thirty-Nine Steps*. In fact, the 1935 film of the book, directed by Alfred Hitchcock, made a much greater feature of the railway element, notably the scene on the Forth Bridge in Scotland, when the police, alerted that Hannay is a fugitive from justice, stop the train on the bridge. It's a great scene but certainly doesn't appear in the book! In *Greenmantle* (1916) Hannay travels on German railways in wartime and in *Mr Standfast* (1919) he uses the Kyle of Lochalsh line on the Highland Railway. Philip Scowcroft in his review of railways in detective fiction states that unlike so many fictional authors, he can't be caught out in a serious railway error, and that 'his railway allusions, never intrusive, are always pleasing'. Sadly, he never seems to have made use of sleeper trains in his thrillers.

We are now at the point when the railway network in Britain was at its most extensive, nearly 20,000 route miles, and technical advances both in engine and carriage design made travelling by rail a comfortable and efficient experience. By 1923 there were nine

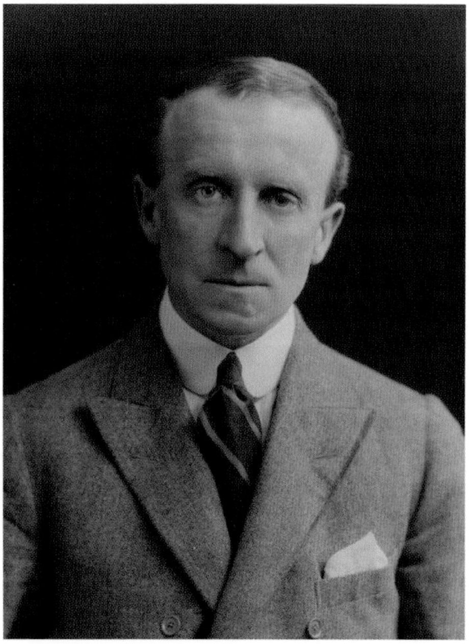

John Buchan, 1st Baron Tweedsmuir (1875–1940). Portrait taken in the 1920s by Elliott and Fry. (National Portrait Gallery)

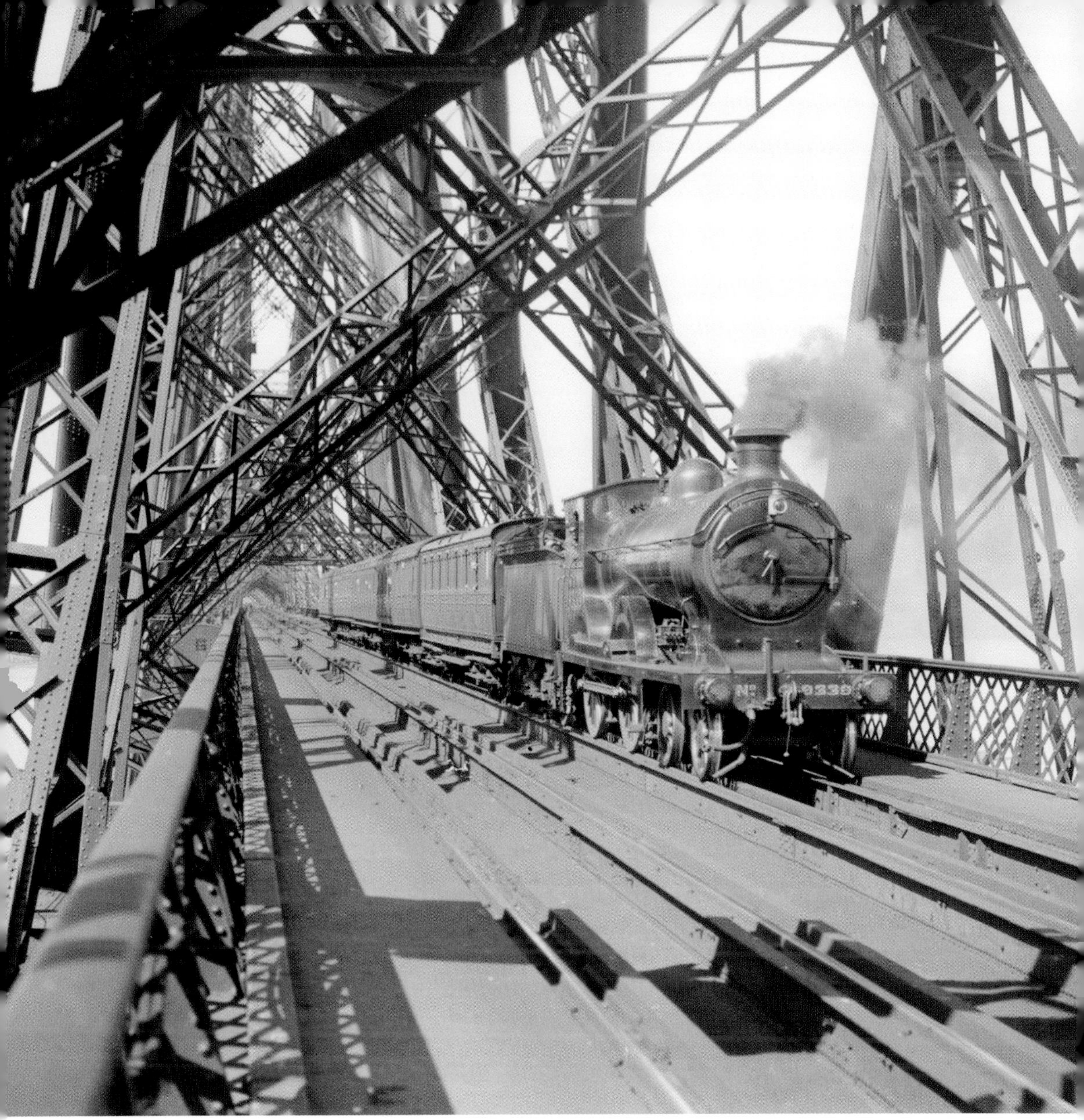

An express train hauled by *Ivanhoe*, an ex-North British Class D 29 4-4-0 locomotive, No. 0330, crossing the Forth Bridge in the years before the Second World War. (Board of Trustees of the Science Museum)

major railways operating in England and five in Scotland. In 1923 these companies were amalgamated to create The Big Four: the London, Midland & Scottish Railway (LMS), the Great Western Railway (GWR), the London & North Eastern Railway (LNER) and the Southern Railway (SR). After the First World War there was a period of intense investment in new steam engines and rolling stock and, spurred on by rising competition from the motor car, strong competition between the 'Big Four' to be the fastest, most modern,

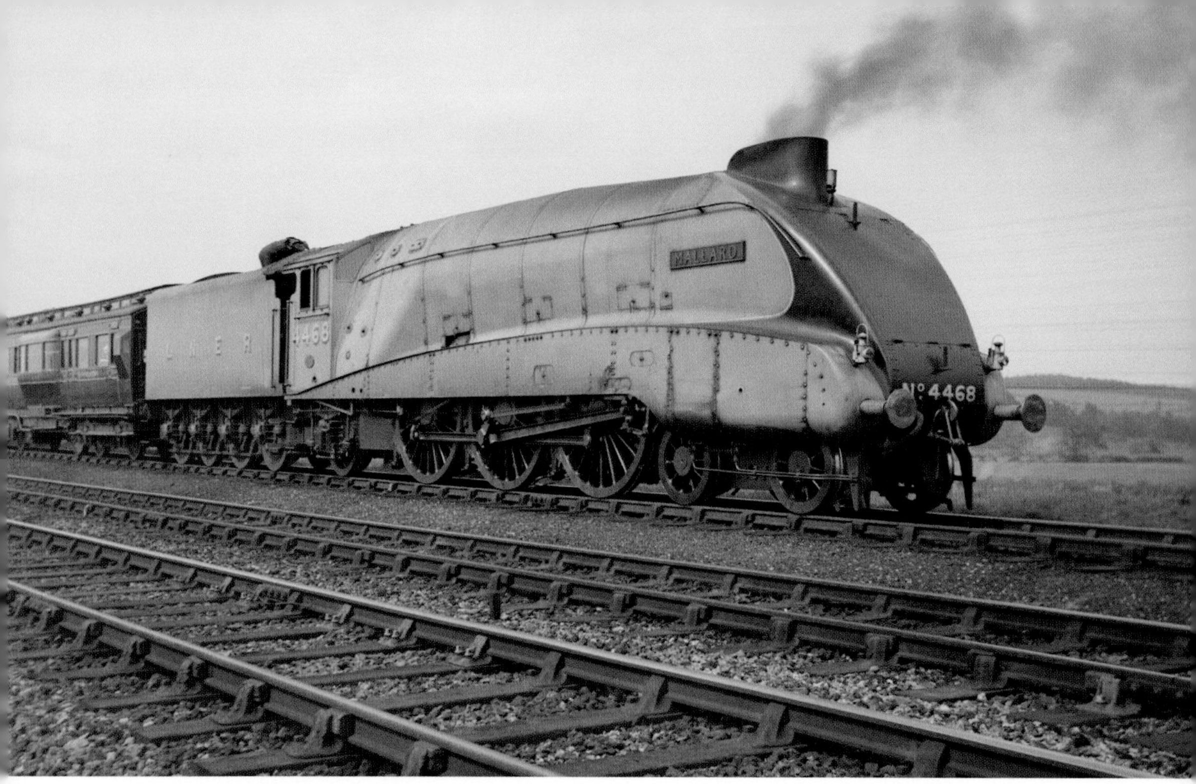

LNER Class A 4 4468 *Mallard* 4-6-2 locomotive, designed by Sir Nigel Gresley and built in 1938, at Barkston Junction before its record run on 3 July 1938. (Board of Trustees of the Science Museum)

luxurious and comfortable trains in Britain. In 1938 the LNER's locomotive *Mallard*, designed by Sir Nigel Gresley, achieved what still remains the land speed record for a locomotive of 126 mph. Elsewhere lines were being electrified, diesel power was being introduced, and slick and stylish marketing became ubiquitous. Many people believe that in the years between the two world wars Britain had the best railway system in the world. The railway, both in Britain and on the Continent, was undoubtedly a prestigious, elegant and comfortable form of travel.

So, gloriously, the Golden Age of Train Travel coincided with what has come to be known as the Golden Age of Detective Fiction, with the result that railways are featured prominently by the writers of this period. Although the age in which they lived and worked has long passed – the age of stylish transatlantic liners, first-class restaurant cars with crisp linen tablecloths and napery, gleaming cutlery and twinkling wine glasses, the age of deference, class consciousness, smart country houses and tweed-suited gentry – nevertheless the genre maintains a powerful hold over our imaginations. In spite of its detractors, the enduring highbrow appeal of the detective novel and spy thriller is one of the literary marvels of our age. Philip Scowcroft has helpfully noted many of the lesser-known writers as well as the big names I have mentioned, including people like John Rhode (aka Major C. J. C. Street, *Death on the Boat Train*, 1940), and Anthony Parsons, *The Mystery of the Cairo Express* (1944).

Another Golden Age author, Henry Holt (1881–1962) wrote twenty-six mystery novels featuring Detective Inspector Jimmy Silver of Scotland Yard. His second story, *The Midnight Mail* (1933), opens on the late-night mail train from Edinburgh via York as it approaches King's Cross in London, seventeen minutes before arrival:

> The great train thundered on, with mails that were due at King's Cross by the stroke of midnight. The guard tapped the ashes out of his pipe, stowed it away in a waistcoat pocket, got up, stretched, yawned. Then he walked into the corridor of the next swaying coach and slid back the door of the nearest compartment.

There he discovers the lifeless body of a young woman. Silver is summoned to the scene and later a man's dead body is discovered 30 miles up the line. Silver doggedly tracks down the perpetrators of this series of murders and robberies, all of which have a connection to the Anglo-American Theatrical Syndicate. This is a high-paced thriller, culminating in a final showdown in a house full of explosives. I particularly liked the throwaway comment of one of the suspects being interviewed by Detective Inspector Silver: 'One is just killing time on a train.' There are also plenty of short stories from this period, including George Radcliffe's *On the Irish Mail* which features a confidence trick played on a LMS Euston to Holyhead Express (anthologised in Dorothy Sayers'

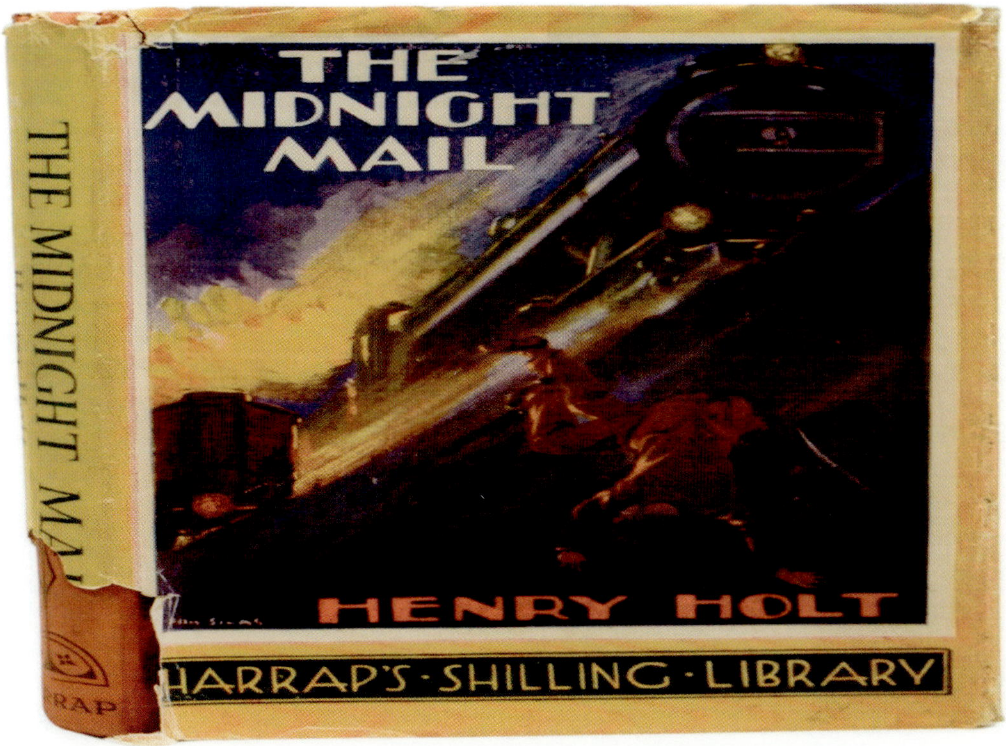

Dust jacket of *The Midnight Mail* by Henry Holt, First Edition, George Harrap & Co., 1933, showing a man falling from the speeding *Night Mail* from Edinburgh to London.

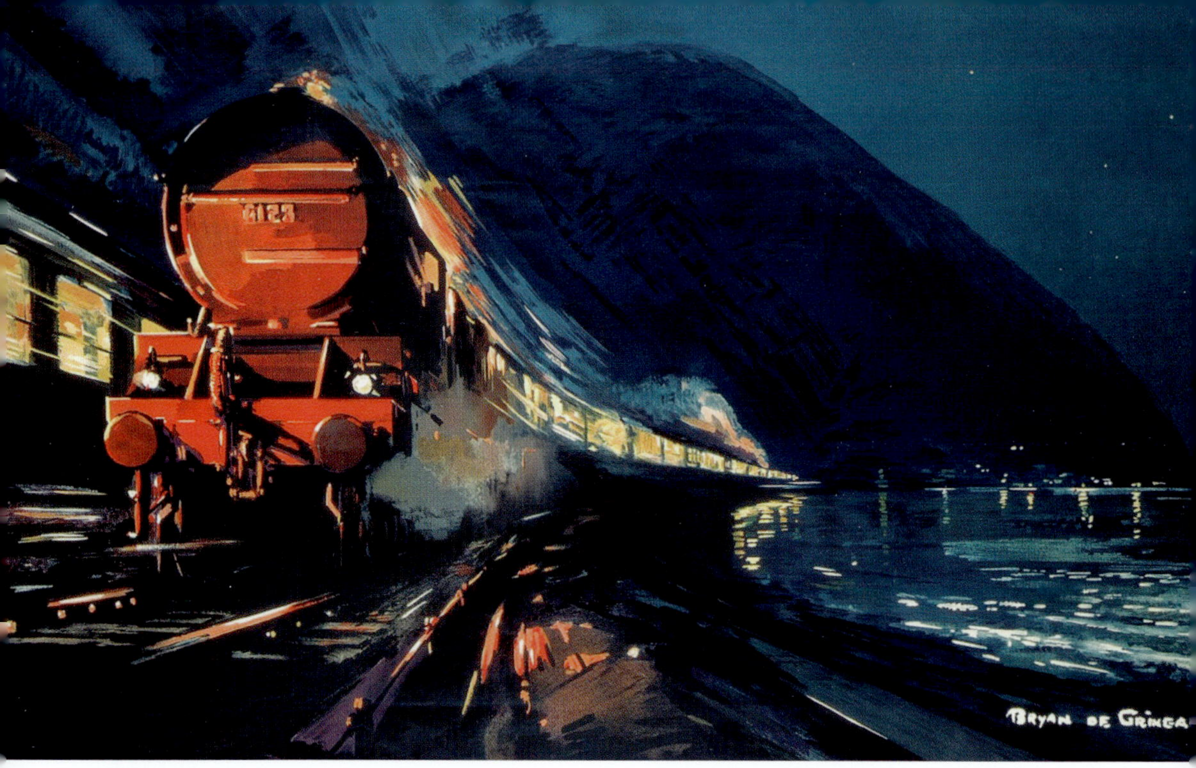

Poster for the Irish Mail, on the London to Holyhead run, passing each other at night. *c.* 1924. Artwork by Bryan de Grineau (1883–1957). Overnight mail trains were famously celebrated in the GPO Film Unit's *Night Mail*, produced in 1936, directed by Harry Watt, with verse by W. H. Auden and music by Benjamin Britten. It was a remarkable fusion of music, verse, sound and cinematography, and was filmed on the LMS London to Scotland Postal Special, pulled by Royal Scot Class No. 6115, *Scots Guardsman.*

Great Short Stories of Detection, Mystery and Horror, 3rd Series, 1934). There were several trains connecting England and Ireland, of which the Irish Mail was probably the most famous. A day train left London Euston at 8.30 a.m. and a night train left at 8.45 p.m. in the evening, both including a Post Office sorting van, and pulled by a 4-6-0 Claughton steam engine. Another named train was the Northern Irishman, which ran overnight from London Euston at 7.10 p.m., using the now-disused line from Dumfries via Newton Stewart to reach Stranraer Harbour at 5.30 a.m. to connect with the 7.00 a.m. ferry to Larne. This train features in one of Freeman Wills Crofts' best detective stories which will be examined in Chapter 2 when the work of some of the major writers of the Golden Age are surveyed.

As the age of steam came to an end in the decades after the Second World War, some of the glamour and romance slipped away from the railways, and this is reflected in the decline of novels set on trains. As Andrew Martin has remarked:

> It's a pity that compartments [in railway carriages] have gone, and it's difficult to imagine meaningfully employing the present-day British railway system in fiction, even as a symbol of anomie ... trains today lack the stand-offish integrity

of old: our stations are shopping centres, our train staff are fluent in the language of PR. Accordingly railway fiction today usually means historical fiction.

Andrew Martin himself has chosen the Edwardian era as the setting for his own novels, which feature his detective Jim Stringer, as in *The Necropolis Railway* (2002). Writer Edward Marston sets his Railway Detective series in the 1850s. However, contemporary railway-based fiction isn't entirely defunct, evidenced by the success of Paula Hawkins' *The Girl on the Train* (2015), a psychological thriller in which a commuting passenger witnesses wrongdoing from her train window and decides to do something about it (an echo of Agatha Christie's *The 4.50 from Paddington*). And we mustn't forget that splendid novella *Tokyo Express* (1958) by Seichō Matsumoto, a novel of train and air timetables, alibis and government corruption, in which two detectives in different cities in Japan work methodically to uncover the murders of a young couple who have travelled on the Tokyo to Hakata daytime express.

Most importantly for the theme of this book, it will be shown that railway fiction that uses night sleeper trains as the setting for murder and mystery is a surprisingly resilient sub-genre because of the continuing romance associated with sleeper trains, even in their modern forms.

Following this brief overview of the role of railway trains in detective fiction, the book proceeds with an account of the enduring popularity of night sleeper trains as the setting for murder, mystery and mayhem in fiction. Each chapter begins with a brief account of the development of the railway system, followed by a chronological account of the murder/mystery fiction associated with overnight sleeper trains.

In Chapter 1 we begin the journey in the United States, where luxury sleeping car travel first began, and look at the development of the railway system across that vast continent which stimulated American writers to add to the genre of Night Sleeper fiction. Then moving eastwards across the Atlantic in Chapter 2 we come back to Britain to examine how our own long-distance sleeper trains have inspired authors of detective and thriller fiction, bringing the narrative right up to the present time with Alexandra Benedict's *Murder on the Christmas Express* (2022), and the mystery thriller TV series *Nightsleeper* (2024), set on the modern overnight Caledonian Sleeper service from Glasgow to London. Even today the night train thriller genre is alive and well and exploring new avenues.

Finally in Chapter 3 we journey further eastwards and examine the glamour of the great Continental sleeper trains immortalised in fiction, beginning with Arthur Griffith's *Rome Express* of 1907 all the way to Ian Fleming's *From Russia with Love* (1957), which was made into the very successful 1963 film by Albert Broccoli and Harry Saltzman, starring Sean Connery as James Bond. We shall examine the stories and look at the real trains portrayed in them, but without giving away details of the solutions to the various murder plots, so that you can go to the novels and enjoy them for yourself.

In many ways this book is a companion volume to my earlier book about the history of Anglo-Scottish sleeper trains, issued by Amberley Publishing in 2018, in which I tried to conjure up the glamour and romance of these long-distance train journeys by night. In that book there were no murders, just a bit of skullduggery concerning drug-dealing, uncovered by a particularly alert cabin crew member on the Highland Line to Inverness. But I wove in lots of stories from those who had travelled on the Scottish routes over the years, which often described unexpected incidents or the times when things went wrong.

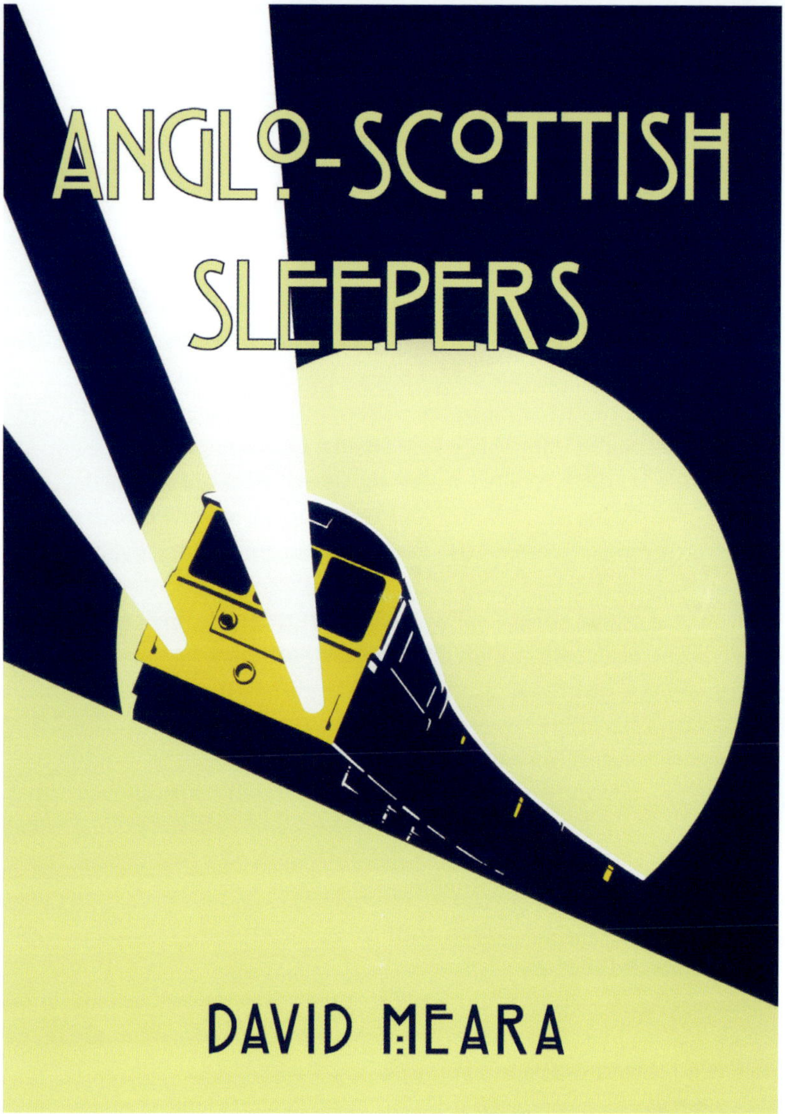

The cover of David Meara's *Anglo-Scottish Sleepers*, 2018, a history of the sleeper service between England and Scotland from 1873 to the present day. The cover is adapted from a 1985 British Railways poster.

There are limitless possibilities for mischief and adventure on a train, especially ones that carry their passengers through the night in locked cabins where anything might happen. This book is copiously illustrated with images from the original books and films, the trains that are represented within them and the journeys they made. I hope that the combination of text and illustrations conjures up the atmosphere of these stories and gives the reader a sense of travelling with their authors as the plots unfold along the railway tracks. There is at the end a bibliography so that readers can follow up the stories that catch their interest and stimulate their imagination.

As the travel writer Paul Theroux wrote in his book *The Great Railway Bazaar*: 'Anything is possible on a train: a great meal, a visit from card players, an intrigue, a good night's sleep ....' And, we might add, a murder to solve or a mystery to unravel.

1

The United States: 'Life is the Train, Not the Station'

As settlements expanded further westwards across the American continent, spurred on by economic promise and a sense of national destiny, there was increasing demand for better communication with the long-settled East Coast. In 1862 President Abraham Lincoln decided to construct a transcontinental railroad, and so the Union Pacific Railroad was born, a line from the tiny settlement of Omaha in Nebraska all the way to the Great Salt Lake Basin, joining up with the Central Pacific Railway. The two lines met at Promontory,

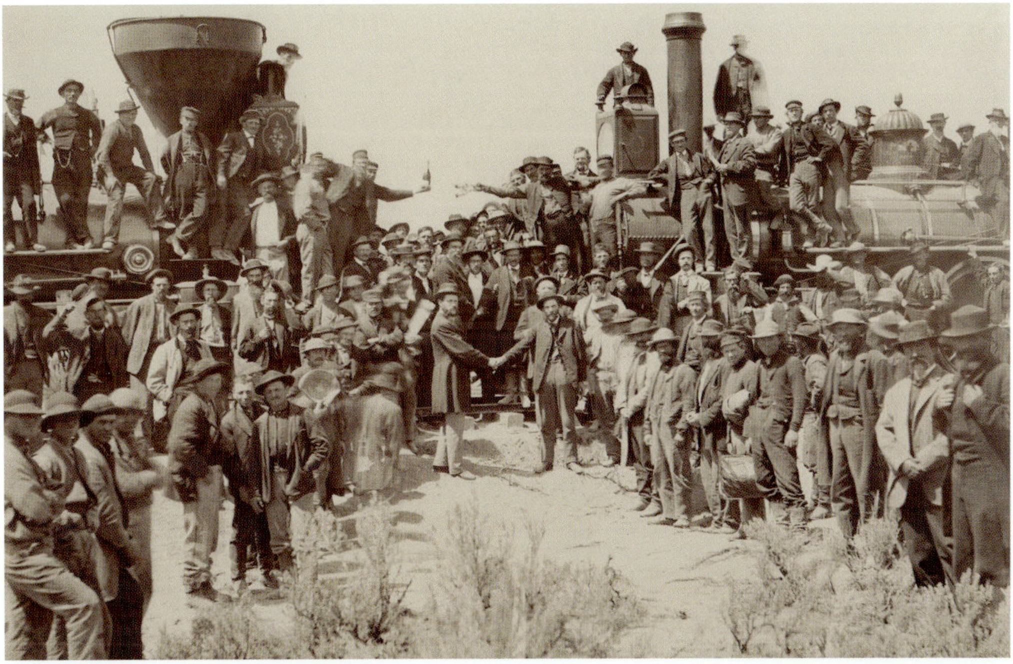

The ceremony of driving the last spike at Promontory Summit, Utah, on 10 May 1869, creating the first transcontinental railroad in the United States. Photographed by Andrew Russell. (Restored by Adam Cuerden)

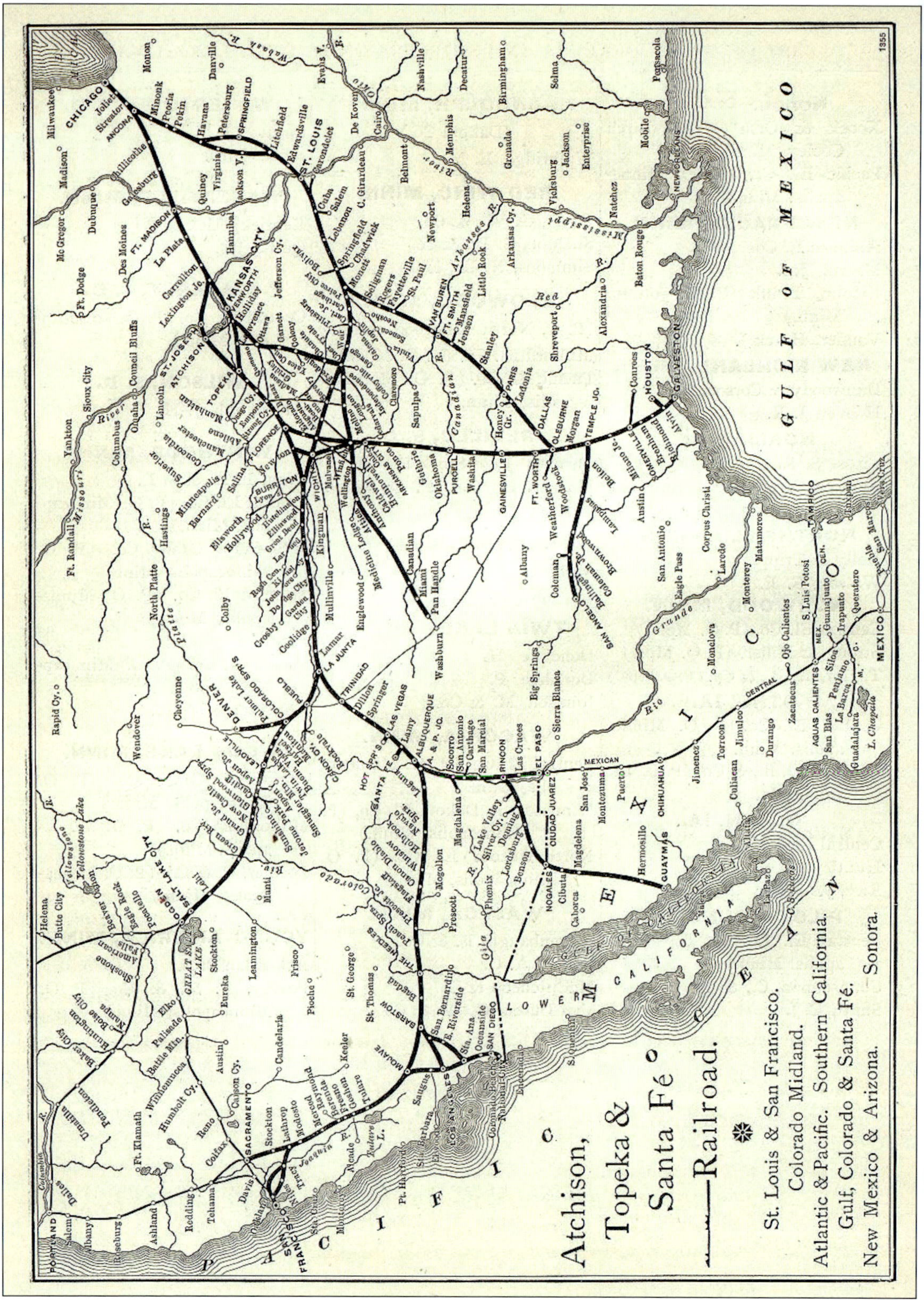
Atchison, Topeka & Santa Fé Railroad.
St. Louis & San Francisco.
Colorado Midland.
Atlantic & Pacific. Southern California.
Gulf, Colorado & Santa Fé.
New Mexico & Arizona. Sonora.
GULF OF MEXICO
PACIFIC OCEAN
MEXICO
LOWER CALIFORNIA
1355

Utah, in May 1869, spanning the country for the first time from coast to coast. Union Pacific boasted a travel time of fifty-nine hours from Chicago to Los Angeles. Soon railroads were being built connecting the main cities of the United States, criss-crossing the continent and covering immense distances.

Between 1871 and 1900 a further 170,000 miles of track were added to the nation's railroad system, providing new economic opportunities and stimulating the development of communities as new towns sprang up along the railway lines. Today, the United States has the largest rail network in the world, but it is 100,000 miles shorter than at its peak in 1917, when 1,500 lines operated over 254,000 miles of track and employed 1.8 million people.

Against this background of a vast and rapidly expanding rail network, we can trace the origins of overnight train travel which began in the United States in August 1859 when a sleeping car appeared on the Chicago & Alton Railroad. The development of this into a luxurious form of overnight travel was the brainchild of one man, George Mortimer Pullman (1831–97), an engineer and industrialist based in Chicago. George Pullman frequently used the railroad network but did not enjoy the experience as he found the carriages uncomfortable and dirty, and the early sleeping cars crude and cramped. So, he decided to build a better and more luxurious version himself, and developed the idea of the Pullman sleeper, or 'palace car'. After President Abraham Lincoln's assassination in April 1865 Pullman cleverly arranged to have his body carried from Washington to Springfield in a sleeping car, and as a result of the publicity orders for his new car began pouring in. In 1867 he introduced his first 'hotel on wheels', The President, a sleeping car with an attached kitchen and dining car, serving high-quality food with impeccable service. During

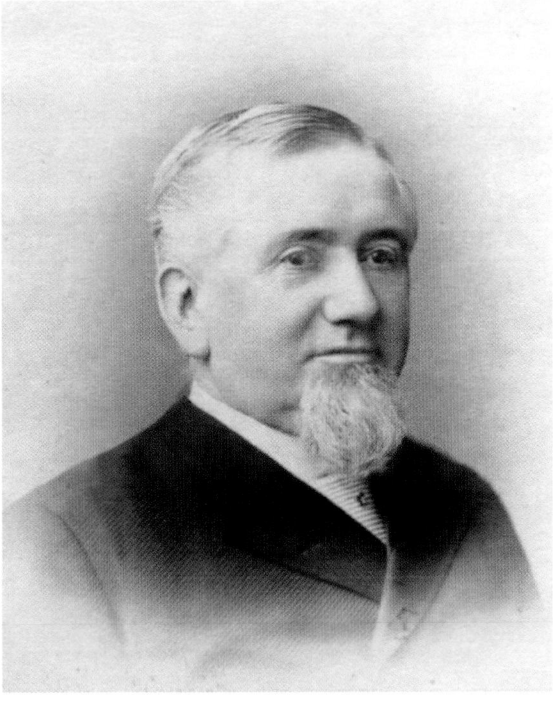

Opposite: Map showing the Atchison, Topeka and Santa Fé railroad route from Chicago to San Francisco, from the 1891 *Grain Dealers and Shippers Gazetteer*. (Wikimedia Commons)

Right: George Mortimer Pullman (1831–97).

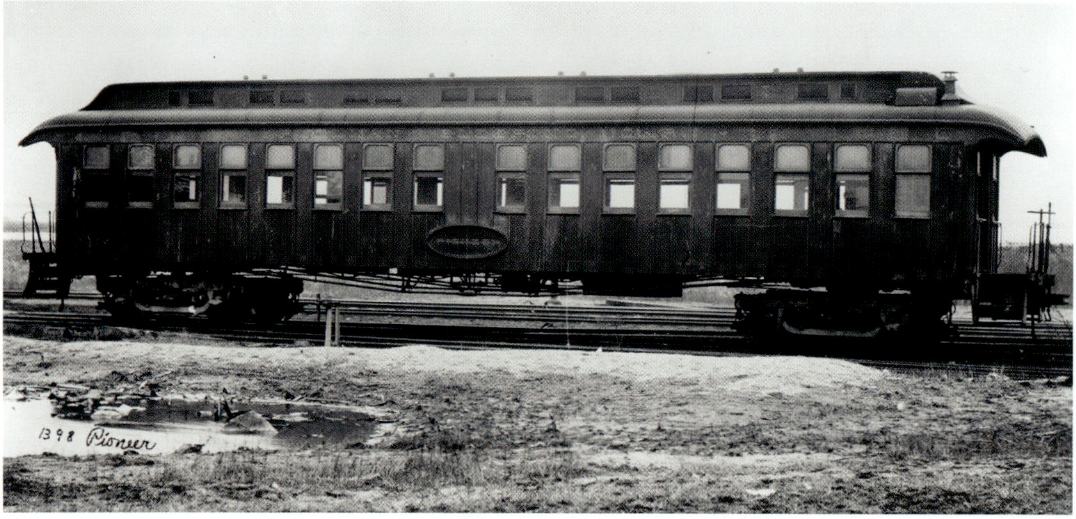

Pullman's prototype sleeping car *Pioneer*, sumptuously fitted out with plush upholstery, velvet curtains, thick carpets, walnut interior and elegant chandeliers.

the day the upper berth was folded up overhead, and at night this was opened up, and the two facing seats below it slid together to create a lower berth. Although far from luxurious, the early Pullman sleepers afforded a degree of comfort and privacy hitherto unknown. By 1875 Pullman had a fleet of 700 sleeping cars, and in 1887 he established carriages linked by vestibules, allowing passengers and crew to move from one carriage to another without getting off the train. Later Pullman cars were refinements of this early design, in which the passengers slept parallel to the direction of travel, unlike in Britain and on the Continent.

If you want an idea of what the layout of these Pullman sleepers looked like, those featured in the 1959 film *Some Like It Hot* are a good example. Starring Marilyn Monroe, Tony Curtis and Jack Lemmon, the protagonists all travel on the sleeper from Chicago to Miami. On either side of the central corridor are rows of bunks, upper and lower, each of them closed off by a pair of curtains, affording minimal privacy. There is a memorable

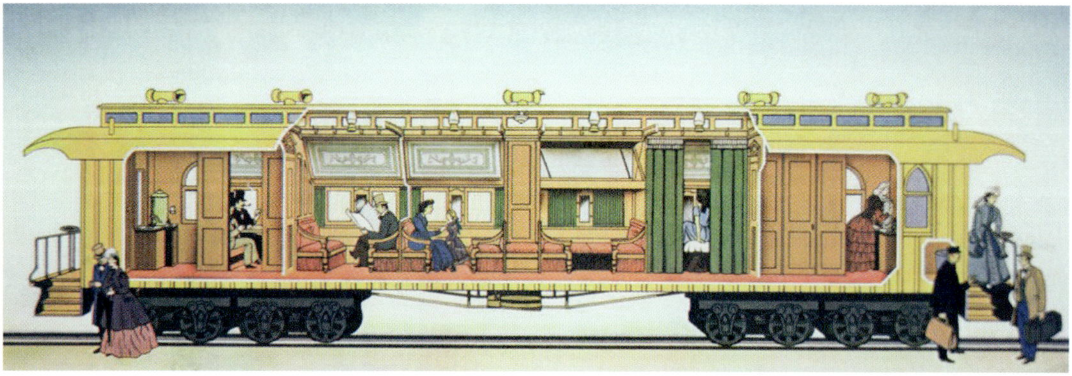

A colour lithograph showing the layout of the interior of a Pullman carriage.

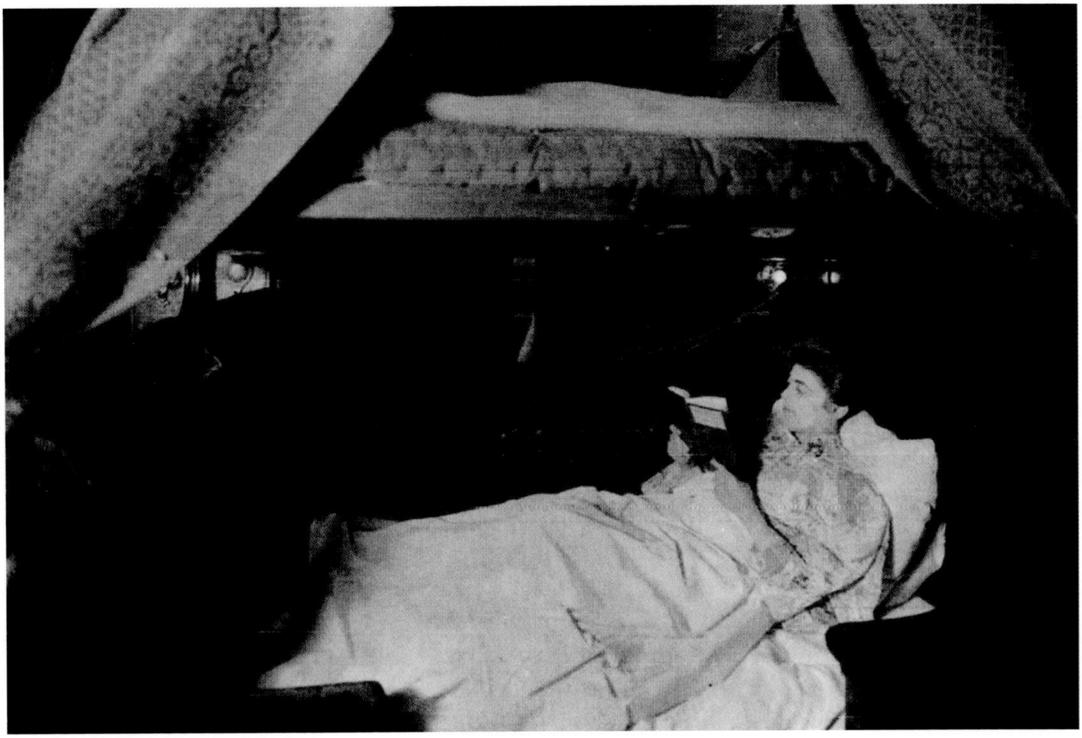

A lady reading in bed in a Pullman sleeping car, *c.* 1905. (Library of Congress, Washington, USA)

night-time party on the train in Bunk No. 7, with Manhattan cocktails mixed in a rubber hot water bottle.

In its heyday Union Pacific ran luxury night expresses across the country, air-conditioned streamliners such as *City of Los Angeles*, *City of San Francisco* and *Portland Rose*. Departing Chicago every evening at 6.30 p.m., the sandy-coloured Pullman cars sported astrodomes and a smart roof-top restaurant car.

One particularly magnificent train was the Orange Blossom Special, which took New Yorkers the 1,390 miles to the tropical shores of Florida in the 1920s and 1930s. It was a magnificent-looking all-electric train with its distinctive green and orange livery. The promotional literature boasted:

> From cheerful club car to spacious observation-car platform, the immaculate Orange Blossom Special emphasises an atmosphere of travel refinement and luxurious comfort.
>
> For gentlemen passengers, valets were on call to ensure 'the well-pressed appearance of one's clothing', while 'expert' barbers offered 'the same service as is obtainable at one's club'. Ladies, meanwhile, were invited to retire to their own lounge where 'the refreshing morning shower and the informal chats, en negligée, are almost a part of the "ritual of dressing"'.
>
> Adrian Bridge, *Daily Telegraph*, 30 December 2024

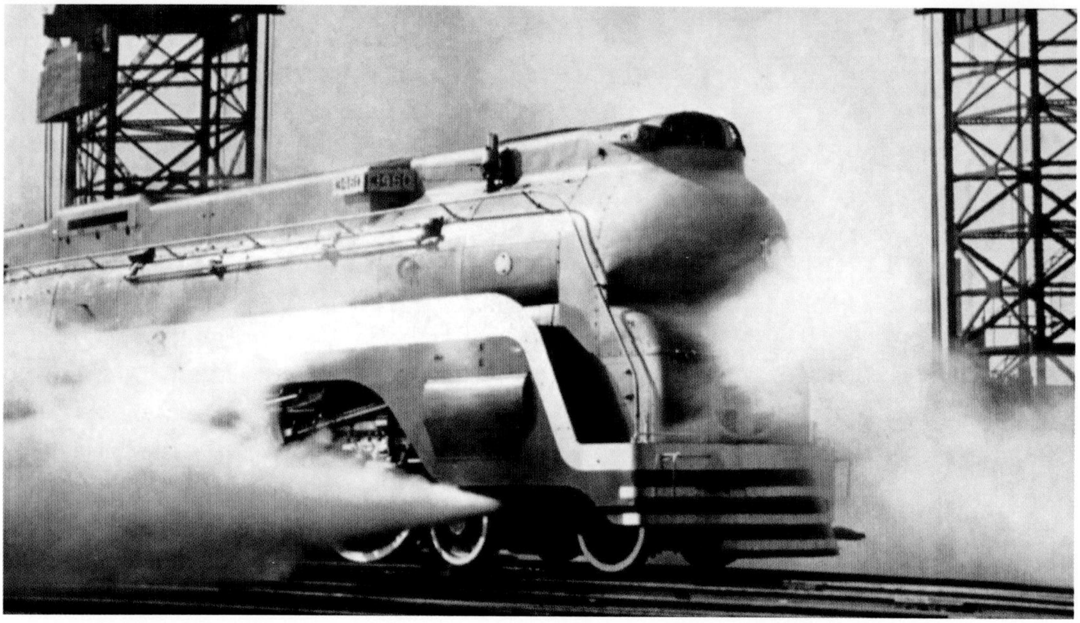

Streamlined steam locomotive 3460, *The Blue Goose,* which hauled The Chief luxury train.

Such luxurious trains, covering vast distances, soon became the settings in which writers of fiction wove their stories, and the murder/mystery genre was no exception. An early example is the short story *A Journey* by the writer Edith Wharton (1866–1937). She was a member of an upper-class family, coming out as a debutante in 1879. She suffered recurrent bouts of illness as a result of an unhappy marriage, and she wrote about this in her published work. Written in the 1890s, *The Journey* is a metaphor for her own unsatisfactory marriage and is set in a Pullman carriage on an overnight train taken by a woman and her dying husband from Colorado to New York.

As they approach New York on the second night he dies in his bunk, but she is too frightened to alert the porter who is anxious to make up the bed in advance of their arrival. She decides to pretend that she doesn't know what has happened, and only to make a scene when the curtains of the bunk are opened. As the train comes into the station through the Harlem Tunnel, the porter makes a final urgent request to get her husband up, she faints and falls, hitting her head against the edge of the bunk, and expires.

In contrast to that dark and sombre tale, contemporary writer William Dean Howells wrote *The Sleeping Car,* a farce in three acts, first published in 1883. The light-hearted action takes place in a Pullman sleeping car on the Boston & Albany Railroad and revolves around a woman's confusion over the unexpected appearance of both her husband and her brother, and is a kind of early bedroom farce about mistaken identity.

These two examples show that the sleeping car could be the setting for both tragedy and comedy, as well as the more straightforward whodunnit. A good example of the latter is *The Problem of the Locked Caboose* by Edward D. Hoch, a classic locked-room mystery featuring Dr Sam Hawthorne, a retired New England physician, and set on a night sleeper train on the Boston & Western Railroad in spring 1925. The Pullman car is next to the caboose

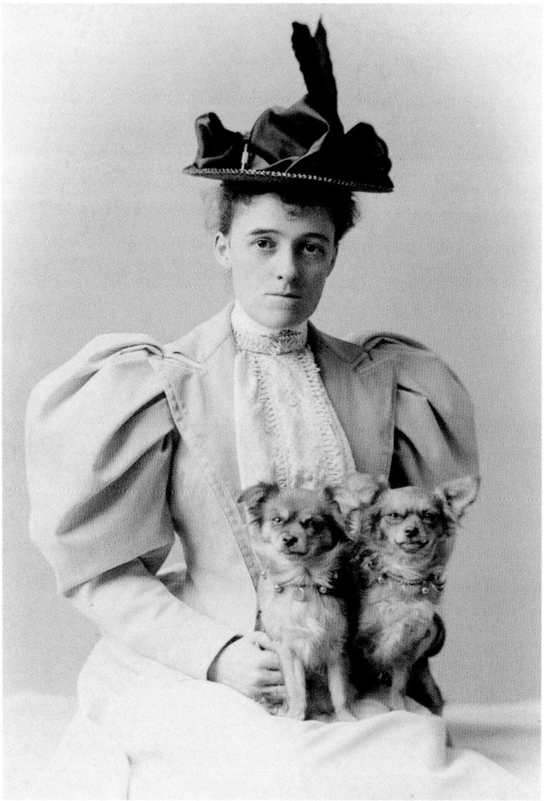

Edith Wharton (1866–1937). Portrait taken by E. F. Cooper at Newport, Rhode Island, USA.

(or luggage van) at the rear of the train. During the journey a guard travelling inside the locked caboose is discovered to have been murdered and the jewellery he was guarding in the safe to have been stolen. Sam Hawthorne, who starred in another seventy-one stories set between 1922 and 1944, solves the crime, while nevertheless enjoying the experience of steam train travel: 'I felt the old thrill that everyone of that era experienced at the arrival of a train – the thrill of being suddenly dwarfed by this massive iron monster that towered above you, all smoking and alive.'

Another prolific American writer of detective fiction in the 1930s was Frederick Nebel (1903–67), who dropped out of school aged fifteen and worked as a dockhand, a valet and as a brakeman on passenger trains, an experience which he put to good use when writing his first novel, *Sleepers East*, published in 1933. The thriller is set entirely on a ten-hour train journey from the Midwest to New York. There is plenty of action and suspense, and the novel was later made into the film *Sleepers West* (1941), itself a remake of an earlier 1934 film of the book.

In the film private detective Michael Shayne secretly escorts a witness in a murder trial, Helen Carson, by overnight train from Denver to San Francisco. Her testimony will free a man falsely accused of murder, but his acquittal will destroy the election chances of a crooked politician. Shayne teams up with his ex-fiancée, Kay Bentley, to keep Helen safe and ensure that she is able to present her testimony in court. The film was praised for its realistic settings on board a train.

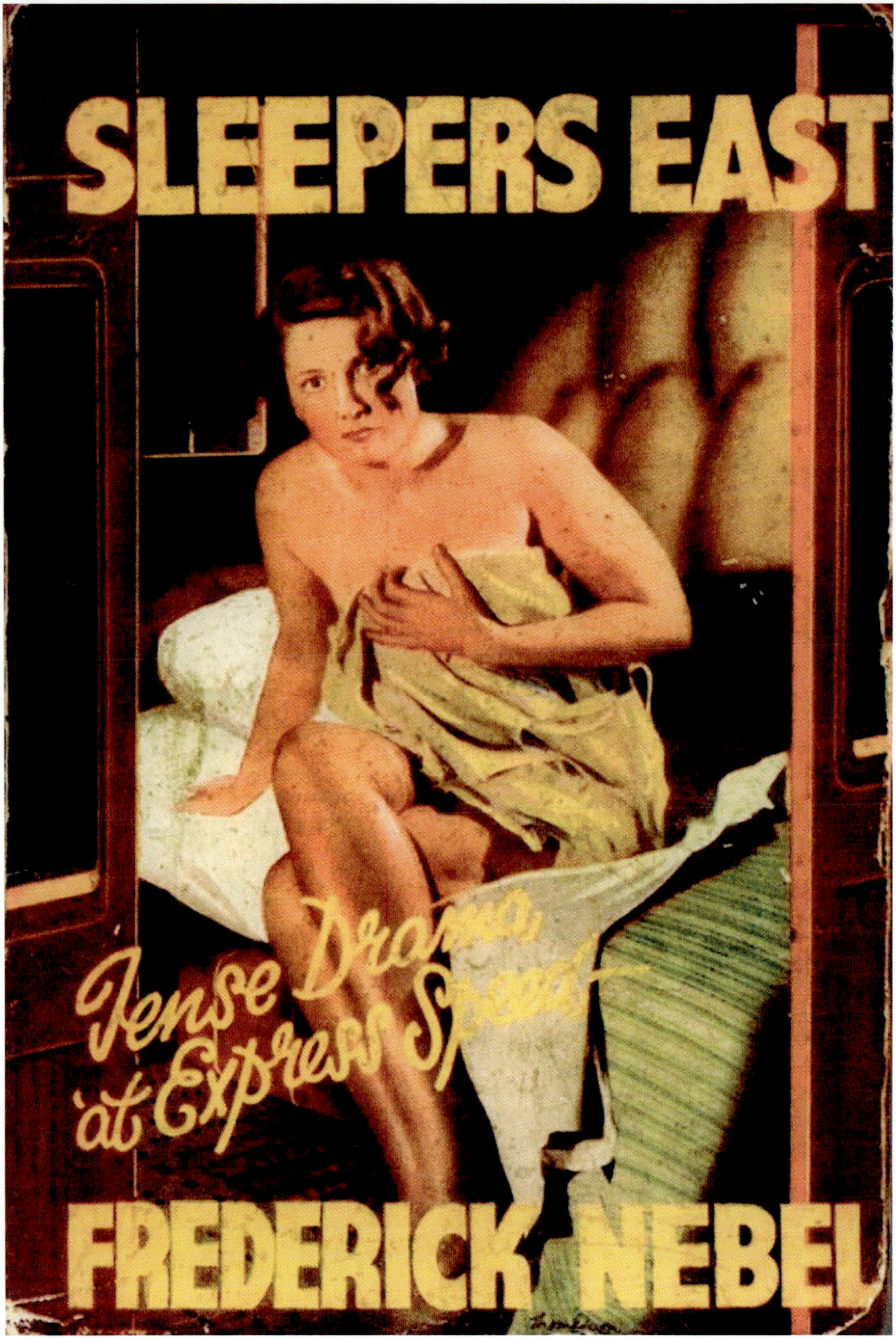

Book cover of *Sleepers East* by Frederick Nebel, 1933. (Author's collection)

A number of railway mystery tales were gathered together in an anthology, *Midnight Specials,* edited by Bill Pronzini and published in 1977. The book gives a fascinating American perspective on the railway murder/mystery genre and includes material from 1870 up to 1975. As well as the stories I have already mentioned you can sample the following: *The Three Good Witnesses* by Harold Lamb, *The Sound of Murder* by William McGivern, *The Train* by Charles Beaumont and a number of other tales, all set on trains. Pronzini also includes a useful bibliography of short stories, novels, plays, films and non-fiction works about the railway, mostly published for the American market. The collection certainly whets the appetite for the material that is available from 'across the pond', as Pronzini himself says:

> If, like me, you are one of those people for whom a train is not just a mode of transportation you will enjoy your journey on these 'midnight specials'. For you'll travel on a variety of passenger, freight and subway trains in this country, in Europe, and in other places strange and wonderful: you'll venture from the early days of railroading through the present and into tomorrow: you'll meet signalmen, hoboes, high balling engineers, foreign correspondents, detectives, thieves, spies and murderers, as well as people just like yourself.

In their heyday, as we have seen, luxury express trains such as The Chief, which ran between Chicago, Illinois, and Los Angeles, California, on the Atchison, Topeka & Santa Fe Railway, carried their passengers in considerable comfort with Pullman sleepers, dining cars, lounge cars and pleasure domes, and became famous as a 'rolling boudoir' for film stars and Hollywood executives. The journey of 2,227 miles was covered in about forty hours in the 1930s travelling through Missouri, New Mexico and the Rocky Mountains, its passengers including stars like Humphrey Bogart, Lauren Bacall, Dean Martin and Judy Garland. The American crime noir writer Dorothy Hughes (1904–93) set her 1945 thriller *Dread Journey* on The Chief as it runs eastwards from Los Angeles to Chicago. She follows a group of passengers travelling on the train who plan to go on to catch the '20th Century' train from Chicago to the East Coast. On board are movie mogul Vivien Spender, his leading star Kitty Agnew, a hard-bitten newspaperman and Gratia, the beautiful starlet whom Spender has chosen to replace Kitty. However, Kitty has incriminating information about Spender and a cast-iron contract and refuses to step aside. When she is discovered dead in her compartment at Kansas, the passengers band together to expose the murderer.

With its luxurious setting this is *The Great Gatsby* on a train. Dorothy Hughes admired the style of Eric Ambler and Graham Greene and gives us a tense and gripping story in which the closed setting of the train ramps up the excitement as each character flounders 'in the inescapable prisons of their own construction'. Against the background of this stylish Pullman sleeper train she deftly exposes the darkness of the celebrity world behind the glamour.

Pronzini put his anthology together just as the American railroad network was beginning its long decline because of competition from the automobile and domestic airlines. Many companies went bankrupt, and the government eventually created Amtrak in 1971 and Conrail in 1976 to manage the system. As a result of these changes much of the

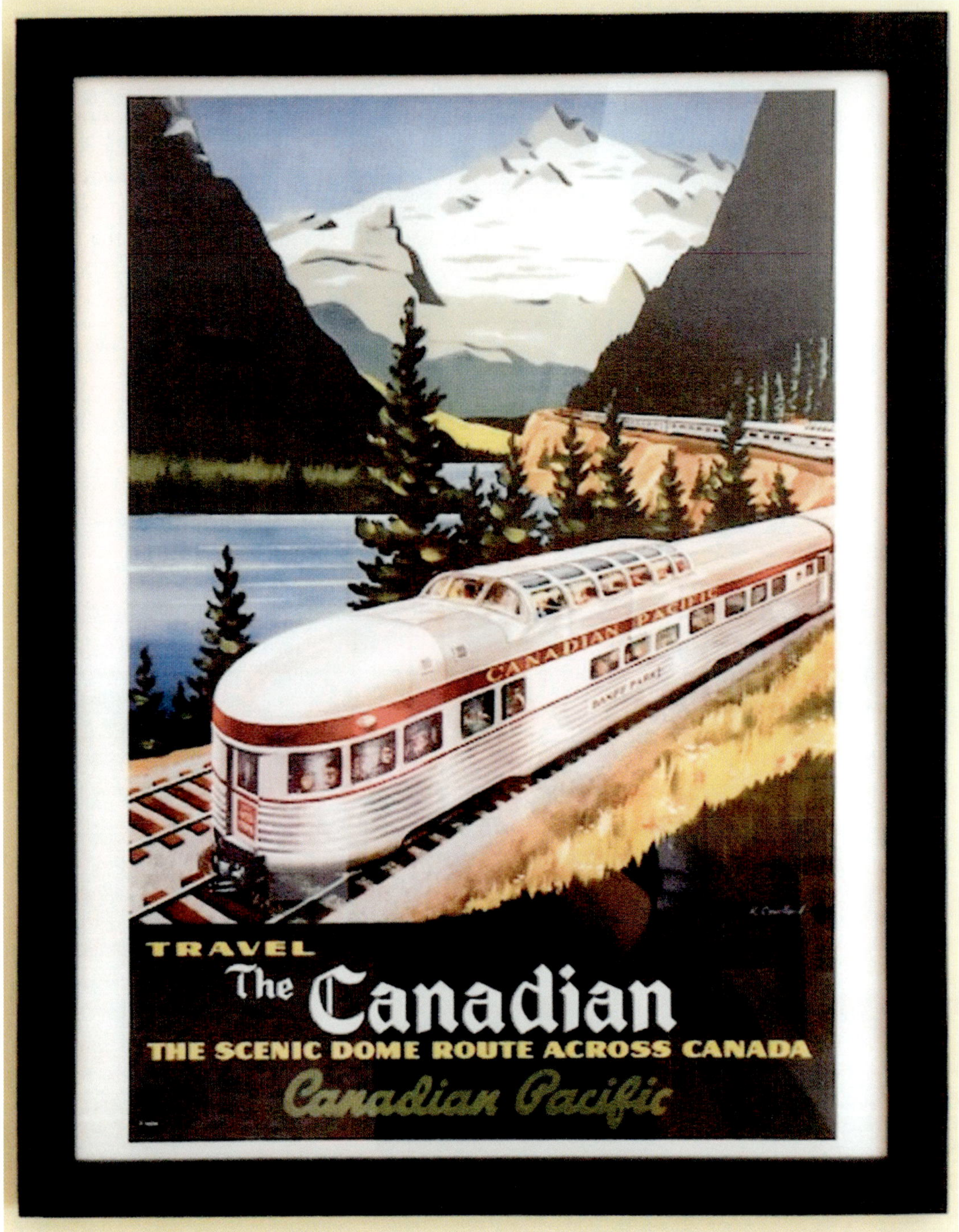

Poster for The Canadian, showing its pleasure dome, as it travels between Toronto and Vancouver.

glamour and romance was lost, and writers looked elsewhere for their settings. However, the genre survives and a good recent example is *The Christmas Train* by David Baldacci, the well-known thriller writer, published in 2003. The story revolves around disillusioned journalist Tom Langdon, who wants to get from Washington DC to Los Angeles in time for Christmas and is forced to take the train. En route Tom meets some intriguing characters, including a mystic, a priest and a movie director, and his journey becomes a mixture of self-discovery, crime investigation and love story. Things keep going missing and there is an investigation by an undercover cop, so this is definitely a crime novel, but there is also lots of information thrown in about Union Pacific trains, they all get stuck in an avalanche on Christmas Eve (shades of Agatha Christie's *Murder on the Orient Express*) and there are a couple of surprises at the end, when love triumphs – well, it is Christmas!

Finally, in this brief survey of the American night sleeper murder/mystery genre, we move north across the border into Canada, the setting for the well-known British thriller writer Dick Francis' (1920–2010) novel *The Edge*, published in 1988. Francis was a former champion jockey who wrote many thrillers about horse racing, and *The Edge* is also set in the racing world.

Tor Kelsey, millionaire detective, travels from Britain to Canada in pursuit of arch villain Julius Filmer, who is suspected of murder, blackmail and intimidation. To gather evidence, he joins a group of wealthy racehorse owners on a luxurious train journey through the Canadian Rockies, the so-called Great Transcontinental Mystery Race Train, which combines fine dining with a murder/mystery game. Disguised as a waiter, Tor has several dangerous encounters with Filmer. As the train runs through the Canadian wilderness from Montreal to Vancouver via Banff and Chateau Lake Louise, a luxury hotel by the shore of Lake Louise, there are backroom deals, dangers, train sabotage, a snowstorm and a touch of romance along the way.

2

Great Britain: 'A Train is a Vehicle that Allows Residence'

Because of the complicated history of railways in Britain there are now two routes to Scotland: the East Coast route, starting from King's Cross, and the West Coast route, which starts from Euston. Historically, there was a third route, operated by the Midland Railway, which opened the Settle and Carlisle line on 1 May 1876, thus allowing through trains to run from St Pancras in London to Glasgow (St Enoch, via Carstairs) and Edinburgh via the Waverley route through the Scottish Borders. The East Coast route – 393 miles to Edinburgh, 47 more to Glasgow – linked together three great railway companies: the Great Northern from King's Cross to Doncaster, the North Eastern from Doncaster to Berwick-on-Tweed and the North British from Berwick to Edinburgh and Glasgow. It is a spectacular line, much better experienced in daylight, taking the traveller through the graceful curve of York station, past Durham with its magnificent cathedral, crossing the Tyne in style at Newcastle, then over the border at Berwick, following the curve of the coast and finally entering the Scottish capital deep in a valley, with Arthur's Seat and the Old Town towering above as the train pulls into Waverley station.

The West Coast route follows the territory of the Midland Railway, later the London Midland & Scottish Railway, which combined the London & North Western Railway, several Scottish railway companies and others to form the LMS under the Railways Act of 1921. It was the largest of the railway companies and served towns and cities from London in the south to Wick in the far north of Scotland.

The grand starting point in London was St Pancras station, which was opened in 1868 by the Midland Railway as the southern terminus of its main lines to the north. The magnificent train shed by William Henry Barlow with its single-span arched roof – the largest such structure in the world at the time of its construction – was a suitably impressive starting point, fronted by the Midland Grand Hotel designed by Sir George Gilbert Scott in flamboyant Italianate Gothic style.

The southern terminus of the West Coast Main Line is now Euston station, which was first built in the 1830s by William Cubitt, and designed by Philip Hardwick. It boasted a Great Hall in the classical style, and an imposing Doric arch as the entrance on Euston Square. Tragically, all this was swept away when the station was rebuilt in a neo-brutalist style in the early 1960s.

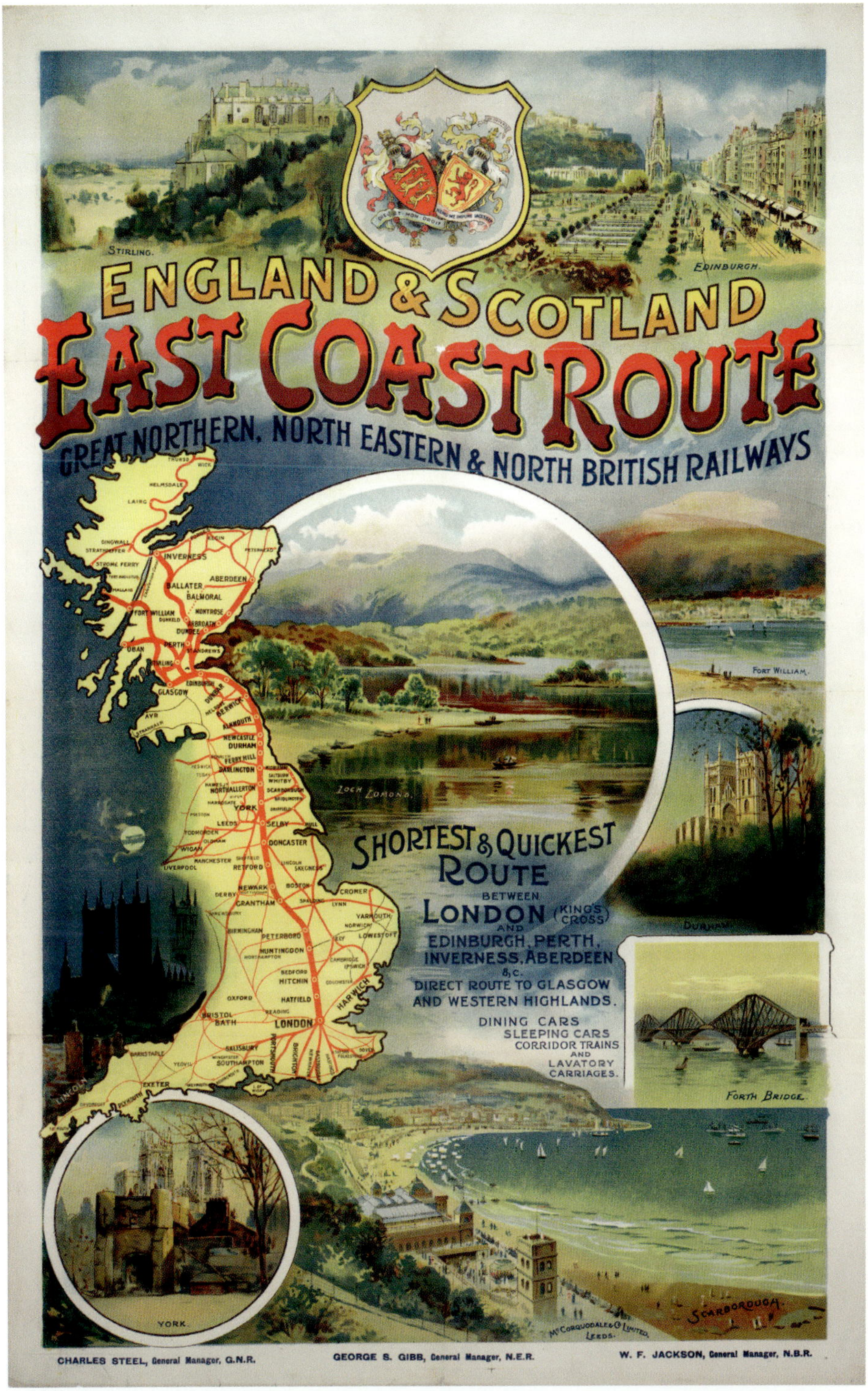

Poster advertising the East Coast route to Scotland, advertising 'Dining Cars, Sleeping Cars, Lavatory Carriages'. It is illustrated with views of York, Lincoln, Durham, the Forth Bridge, Edinburgh and Fort William. (Author's collection)

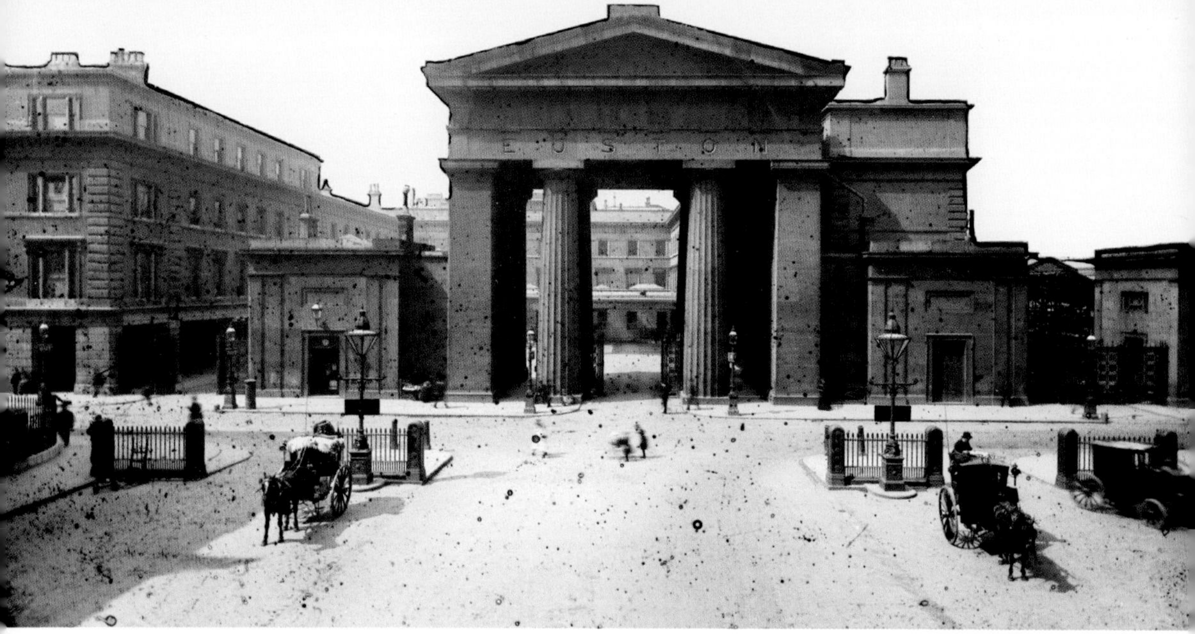

The Euston arch and Euston station, 1898. Euston was the first London terminus to be built, opening in 1838. The arch was designed by Philip Hardwick in the Doric style and demolished in 1962. (Board of Trustees of the Science Museum)

These, then, are the routes on which Victorian passengers would have travelled when visiting Scotland for business or pleasure. Apart from an early 'Bed Carriage' which was attached to the Royal Train for Queen Adelaide, the widow of King William IV, in 1842, the first sleeping car designed for the general public appeared in 1873, attached to a North British Railway service between Glasgow and London. It was a six-wheel carriage, a plush affair with polished walnut interiors, ebony and brass fittings and carpets. It wasn't popular at first because the Victorians didn't like the idea of taking their clothes off in public, but the concept gradually took hold, spurred on by the introduction of Pullman sleeping cars on the Midland Railway in 1874.

This was the brainchild of James Allport, General Manager of the Midland Railway, who had toured America and was very impressed with George Mortimer Pullman's new sleeping cars. Pullman offered to build cars suitable for the British loading gauge, and to ship them over to England. By June 1874 the first sleeping car, named *Midland,* was running on Midland Railway lines between Bradford and London St Pancras. But these Pullman cars never really caught on because British passengers didn't like the open saloon style, and when the agreement with Pullman expired in 1888, the Midland Railway began designing their own carriages. Instead of the American layout, sleeping cars designed in Britain adopted the transverse sleeping berth in separate compartments opening onto a side corridor, and that arrangement has become the norm both in Britain and on the Continent ever since.

In 1877 the first sleeping car on the Great Western Railway was introduced, running from London Paddington to Plymouth using 7-ft, broad-gauge carriages with seven gentlemen's and four ladies' berths. By 1881 this layout had been replaced by carriages with individual

Queen Adelaide's bed carriage, 1840. A large cushion on the floor supported the mattress. (Board of Trustees of the Science Museum)

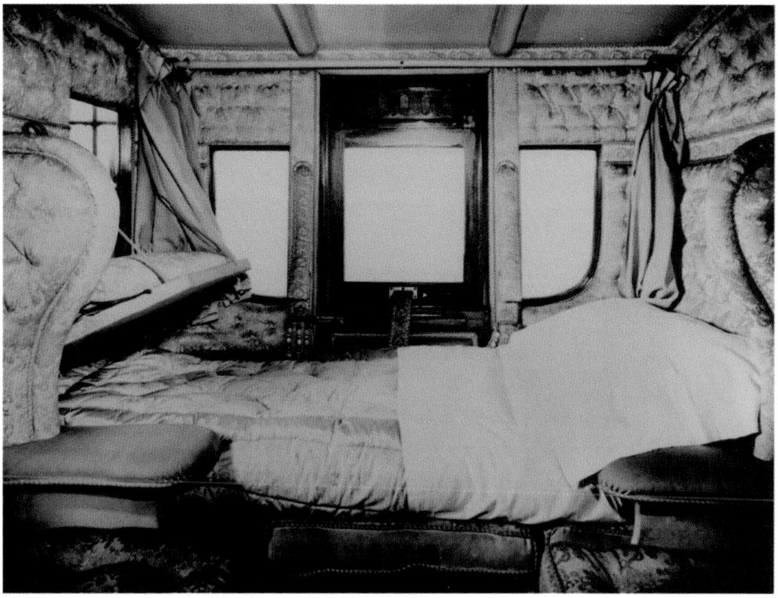

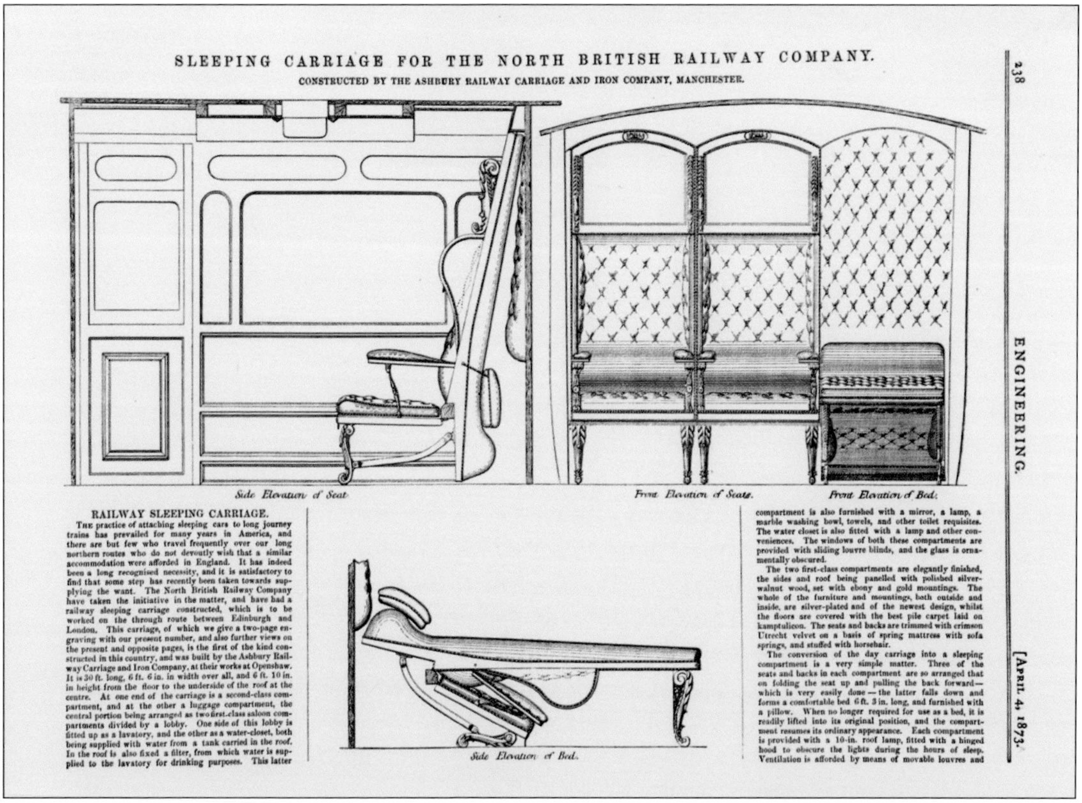

238 ENGINEERING. [April 4, 1873.

SLEEPING CARRIAGE FOR THE NORTH BRITISH RAILWAY COMPANY.

CONSTRUCTED BY THE ASHBURY RAILWAY CARRIAGE AND IRON COMPANY, MANCHESTER.

Side Elevation of Seat. *Front Elevation of Seats.* *Front Elevation of Bed.* *Side Elevation of Bed.*

RAILWAY SLEEPING CARRIAGE.

The practice of attaching sleeping cars to long journey trains has prevailed for many years in America, and there are but few who travel frequently over our long northern routes who do not devoutly wish that a similar accommodation were afforded in England. It has indeed been a long recognised necessity, and it is satisfactory to find that some step has recently been taken towards supplying the want. The North British Railway Company have taken the initiative in the matter, and have had a railway sleeping carriage constructed, which is to be worked on the through route between Edinburgh and London. This carriage, of which we give a two-page engraving with our present number, and also further views on the present and opposite pages, is the first of the kind constructed in this country, and was built by the Ashbury Railway Carriage and Iron Company, at their works at Openshaw. It is 30 ft. long, 6 ft. 6 in. in width over all, and 6 ft. 10 in. in height from the floor to the underside of the roof at the centre. At one end of the carriage is a second-class compartment, and at the other a luggage compartment, the central portion being arranged as two first-class saloon compartments divided by a lobby. One side of this lobby is fitted up as a lavatory, and the other as a water-closet, both being supplied with water from a tank carried in the roof. In the roof is also fixed a filter, from which water is supplied to the lavatory for drinking purposes. This latter compartment is also furnished with a mirror, a lamp, a marble washing bowl, towels, and other toilet requisites. The water closet is also fitted with a lamp and other conveniences. The windows of both these compartments are provided with sliding louvre blinds, and the glass is ornamentally obscured.

The two first-class compartments are elegantly finished, the sides and roof being panelled with polished silver-walnut wood, set with ebony and gold mountings. The whole of the furniture and mountings, both outside and inside, are silver-plated and of the newest design, whilst the floors are covered with the best pile carpet laid on kamptulicon. The seats and backs are trimmed with crimson Utrecht velvet on a basis of spring mattress with sofa springs, and stuffed with horsehair.

The conversion of the day carriage into a sleeping compartment is a very simple matter. Three of the seats and backs in each compartment are so arranged that on folding the seat up and pulling the back forward—which is very easily done—the latter falls down and forms a comfortable bed 6 ft. 3 in. long, and furnished with a pillow. When no longer required for use as a bed, it is readily lifted into its original position, and the compartment resumes its ordinary appearance. Each compartment is provided with a 10-in. roof lamp, fitted with a hinged hood to obscure the lights during the hours of sleep. Ventilation is afforded by means of movable louvres and

A drawing of the interior of the first sleeping carriage, 1873, built for the North British Railway, showing how the daytime seats converted into sleeper use by folding the seat up and pulling the back forward, making a respectable 6-ft 3-in bed. (Author's collection)

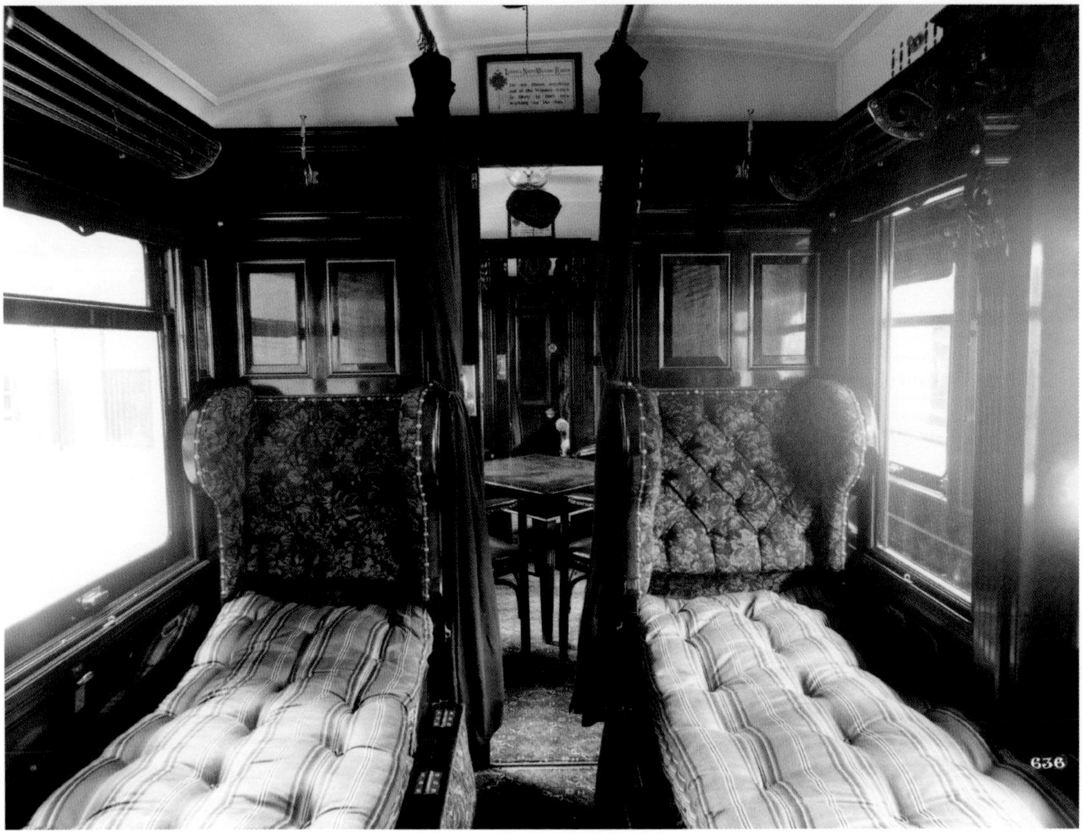

An early LMS Pullman carriage with the seats made into beds, *c.* 1920. (Board of Trustees of the Science Museum)

compartments. An additional service was soon added to Penzance, the forerunner of the Night Riviera, which features briefly in one of Freeman Wills Crofts' detective novels.

It didn't take long after the introduction of sleeping cars for them to begin appearing in contemporary literature. In *The Rajah's Diamond,* a short story by Robert Louis Stevenson published in 1878, a clergyman flees to Scotland with a stolen precious stone on what is clearly a North British sleeper. In the latter years of the nineteenth century there was intense rivalry between the railway companies to run the fastest services to Scotland, each vying to show that the West Coast route via Carlisle (540 miles to Aberdeen) or the East Coast route via Newcastle on Tyne (523 miles to Aberdeen) was the best and fastest.

The competition reached a climax in 1895 when the expresses competed in what came to be known as 'The Race to the North'. The big players, the LMS and the LNER, were egged on by the newspapers to beat their rival, until an inspector, horrified that speed limits over the recently opened Forth and Tay bridges were being ignored, called a halt to the races. The Race to the North makes an appearance in one of Canon Victor Whitechurch's short stories, *A Perilous Ride,* which we shall examine later. Sleeping-car design developed rapidly during the early years of the twentieth century, so that by the inter-war years, the Golden Age of Train Travel, night trains had become a stylish and sophisticated form of transport, with

Right: The Golden Arrow leaving Victoria station in 1953, pulled by Britannia Class 7 4-6-2 No. 70004, *William Shakespeare*. (Ben Brooksbank)

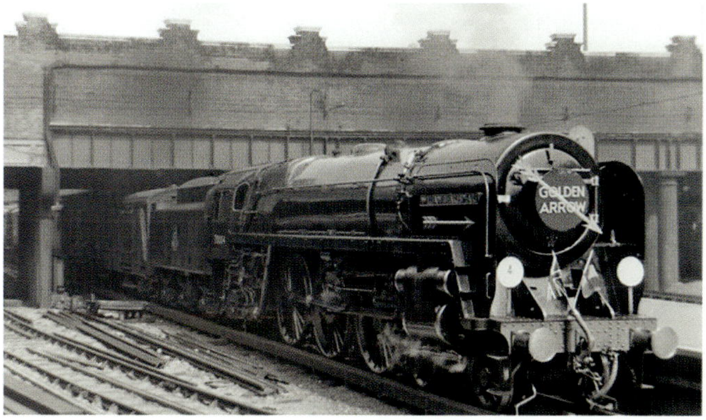

Below: British Rail Southern Region poster 'Bon Voyage', from a painting by Terence Cuneo, 1952, showing SS *Invicta* and SS *Cote D'Azur* berthed at Calais harbour with boat trains waiting at the pier.

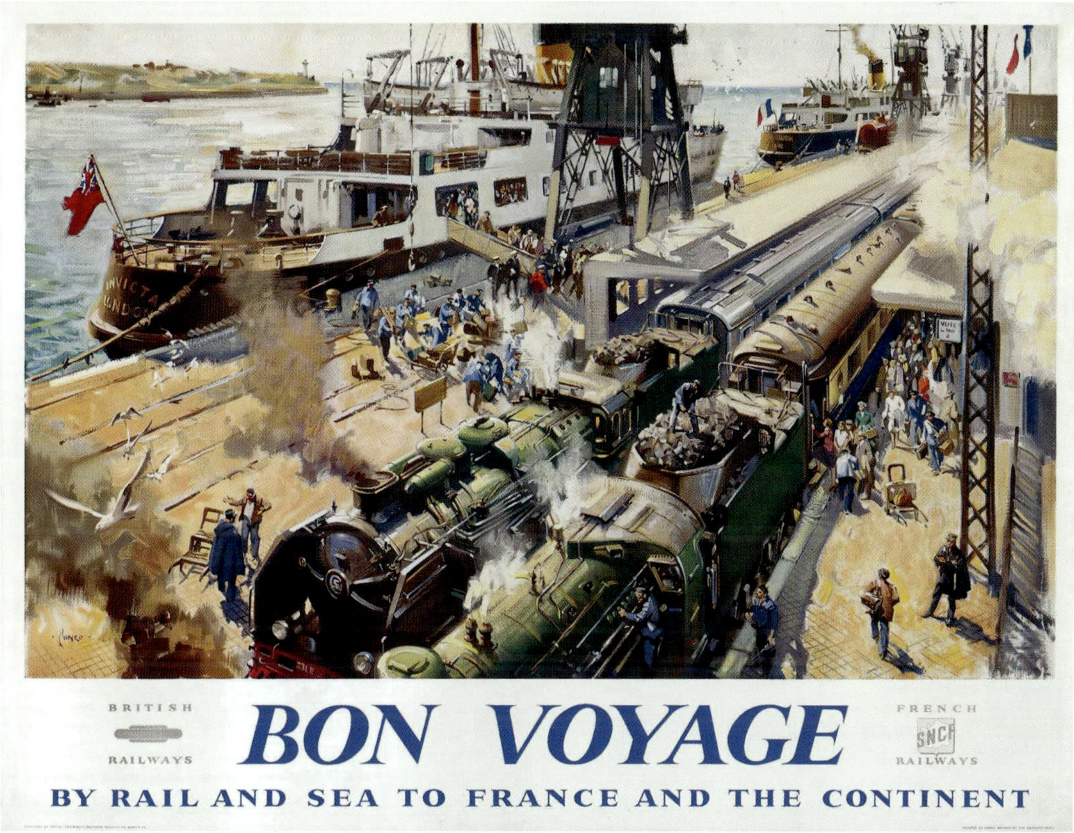

named trains like the Royal Highlander, the Aberdonian and the Night Scot running between London and Scotland, and the Golden Arrow taking passengers across the Channel to France.

The service on these overnight trains was first class only to preserve the exclusive nature of the operation. The LNER designed particularly luxurious sleeping carriages, with well-sprung beds, individual sitting rooms and shower compartments. The service was promoted via stylish poster campaigns, adding to the sense of glamour and exclusivity.

SLEEPING CAR EXPRESSES

FIRST AND SECOND CLASS SLEEPING ACCOMMODATION IS PROVIDED BY TRAINS RUNNING VIA THE "EAST COAST" ROUTE BETWEEN ENGLAND AND SCOTLAND AS UNDER:—

WEEK DAYS

		F	J	F		E	S	E	S	E	S	E	E	S	S
	THE TYNESIDER		THE ABERDONIAN	THE ABERDONIAN			Second class only						THE NIGHT SCOTSMAN First class only	THE NIGHT SCOTSMAN	THE TYNESIDER
	am	pm	pm	pm		pm	pm	pm	pm	pm	pm	pm	pm	pm	pm
LONDON (King's Cross) dep	1Y 0	7 30	7 30	7 45	..	9 50	9 50	10 15	10 15	10 30	10 30	11G20	11L35	11L35	11H55
Peterborough (North) .. „	..	..	..	..	..	..	..	..	..	am	am	..			1a29
Grantham „	..	9 35	9 41	9 56	..	11 54	11 54	..	..	12 35	12 35	..			2 15
Newark (North Gate) .. „	..	..	..	..	..	am	am	..	..	..	..	..			2 38
Doncaster „	..	..	..	..	..	1 4	1 10	..	..	..	..	..			3 35
York „	..	11 24	11 30	11 45	..	..	..	..	..	2 25	2 25	..			4 34
Darlington arr	5A26	..	12a22	12a37	..	..	..	..	..	3 17	3 17	..			5 26
Ferryhill „	..	..	..	..	..	..	..	..	..	..	..	..			5 57
Durham „	6 5	am	..	..	..	..	..	..	..	..	..	am			6 9
Newcastle „	6A31	1 1	1 14	1 29	..	3 21	3 31	..	..	4 10	4 10	4 28			6A35
Morpeth „	7K23	..	..	..	..	..	..	..	..	..	..	..	..	..	..
Acklington „	7K45	..	..	..	..	..	..	..	..	..	..	..	..	..	..
Alnmouth „	7K55	..	..	..	..	..	..	..	..	..	..	..	..	..	..
Longhoughton „	8K 4	..	..	..	..	..	..	..	..	..	..	..	..	..	..
Berwick-upon-Tweed .. „	8K37	..	..	..	..	..	..	..	..	5 36	5 36	..	..	..	..
Dunbar „	9K12	..	..	..	..	..	..	..	..	..	..	..	..	..	..
Drem „	..	..	..	..	..	..	..	..	..	..	C	B	am	am	..
Edinburgh (Waverley) ... „	9K46	3 32	3 45	4 1	..	5c52	6b 3	..	..	6 45	6 50	7A 5	7A18	7A17	..
Fort William „	..	..	10D12	9 53	..	..	..	am	am	..	..	..	..	..	..
Dundee (Tay Bridge) .... „	..	5 23	5N30	5 51	..	8 37	..	7 36	8 4	..	..	..	..	..	..
Arbroath „	..	5 54	6N 1	6 22	..	..	..	8 7	8 35	..	..	..	..	..	..
Montrose „	..	6 18	6N25	6 46	..	..	..	8 32	8 59	..	..	..	..	..	..
Aberdeen „	..	7 21	7N28	7 49	..	..	..	9 31	10 5	..	..	..	..	..	..

WEEK DAYS

		J		S	E		F	M							E	S	
	THE TYNESIDER			First class only				Second class only				THE NIGHT SCOTSMAN			THE ABERDONIAN	THE ABERDONIAN	
	pm	pm		pm	pm		pm	pm		pm		pm		pm	pm	pm	
Aberdeen dep	..	..	..	..	..	..	..	..	..	..	..	..	..	7 5	8 30	8 30	..
Montrose „	..	..	..	..	..	..	..	..	..	..	..	..	..	8 5	9 32	9 32	..
Arbroath „	..	..	..	..	..	..	..	..	..	..	..	..	..	8 28	9 54	9 54	..
Dundee (Tay Bridge) .... „	..	..	..	..	..	..	..	..	..	..	..	..	..	9 1	10 25	10 25	..
Fort William „		..	..	..	..	..	..	..	..	..	..	4V40	..	..	..	..	..
Edinburgh (Waverley) .. „		..	..	..	..	..	..	10 10	..	10 30	..	10 50	..	11 5			..
Drem „		..	..	..	8 30	..	..	..	..	..	..		..	..			..
Dunbar „		..	..	..	8 45	..	..	..	..	..	..		..	..			..
Berwick-upon-Tweed .. „		..	..	..	9 26	..	..	..	..	11 41	..		..	..			..
Belford „		..	..	..	9 46	..	..	..	..	..	..		..	..			..
Chathill „		..	..	..	9 56	..	..	..	..	..	..		..	..			..
Alnmouth „		..	..	..	10 14	..	..	..	..	..	..		..	..			..
Morpeth „		..	..	..	10 39	..	..	am	..	am	..		..	am			..
Newcastle „	10 45	10 25	..	11 20	11K20	..	11 5	12U40	..	1U 7	..		..	1U37			..
Sunderland „	..	10 50	..	..	..	..	11 31	..	..	..	..		..	..			..
West Hartlepool „	..	11 23	..	..	..	..	12a 4	..	..	..	..		..	..			..
Stockton „	..	11 51	..	..	..	..	12 30	..	..	..	..		..	..			..
Durham „	11 7	..	..	11 45	11K45	..	..	..	..	..	..		..	..			..
Ferryhill „	..	..	..	12a 3	am	..	..	..	..	..	..	..	..	..	..	..	..
Darlington „	11 45	am	..	12 28	12Z22	..	..	..	..	..	..	am	..	..	am	am	..
York „	am	1 2	..	1 23	1Z20	..	1 39	..	..	..	..	..	..	..	..	..	..
Doncaster arr	..	1 45	..	2 6	2 3	..	2 22	..	..	..	..	..	..	3 55	..	..	..
Grantham „	..	2 50	..	3 14	3 14	..	3 36	3 49	..	..	..	..	..	4 59	..	..	..
Peterborough (North) .. „	..	..	..	3 57	3 57	..	..	..	..	..	..	..	..	5 37	..	..	..
LONDON (King's Cross) „	4‡20	5‡ 5	..	5 40	5§40	..	6‡ 0	6†10	..	6 20	..	6*40	..	7 20	7 47	8 12	..

Arrival times—Tuesday to Sunday mornings inclusive

SUNDAYS

	THE ABERDONIAN										THE NIGHT SCOTSMAN First class only		Second class only		
	pm		pm		pm		pm		pm		pm		pm		
LONDON (King's Cross) dep	7 30	..	9 50	..	10 15	..	10 25	..	11G20	..	11L35	..	11H45	..	..
Peterborough (North) .. „	..	..	..	..	..	..	am	..	..	..	..	..	am	..	..
Grantham „	9 41	..	11 54	..	..	..	12 32	..	..	..	..	..	1 50	..	..
Doncaster „	..	..	1a 4	..	..	..	..	..	..	..	..	..	..	..	..
York „	11 30	..	..	..	..	..	2 14	..	..	..	..	..	3 46	..	..
Darlington arr	12a22	..	..	..	..	..	3 7	..	..	..	..	..	4 38	..	..
Ferryhill „	..	..	..	..	..	..	..	..	..	..	..	..	5 3	..	..
Durham „	..	..	..	..	..	..	..	..	am	..	..	..	5 21	..	..
Newcastle „	1 14	..	3 21	..	..	..	4 2	..	4 28	..	..	..	5A47	..	..
Alnmouth „	..	..	..	..	..	..	..	..	..	..	..	..	..	..	..
Berwick-upon-Tweed .. „	..	..	..	..	..	..	5 29	..	..	..	..	..	..	..	..
Drem „	..	..	..	..	..	..	..	..	B	..	am	..	..	..	..
Edinburgh (Waverley) .. „	3 45	..	5c52	..	..	..	6 38	..	7A 5	..	7A18	..	..	..	..
Fort William „	10 12	..	..	..	am	..	..	..	..	..	..	..	..	..	..
Dundee (Tay Bridge) .. „	5 30	..	8 37	..	7 36	..	..	..	..	..	..	..	..	..	..
Arbroath „	6 1	..	..	..	8 7	..	..	..	..	..	..	..	..	..	..
Montrose „	6 25	..	..	..	8 32	..	..	..	..	..	..	..	..	..	..
Aberdeen „	7 28	..	..	..	9 31	..	..	..	..	..	..	..	..	..	..

FOR CONTINUATION OF SUNDAY TRAINS AND NOTES, SEE PAGE 43

A British Rail timetable from the 1950s showing named trains operating between London and Scotland. (Author's collection)

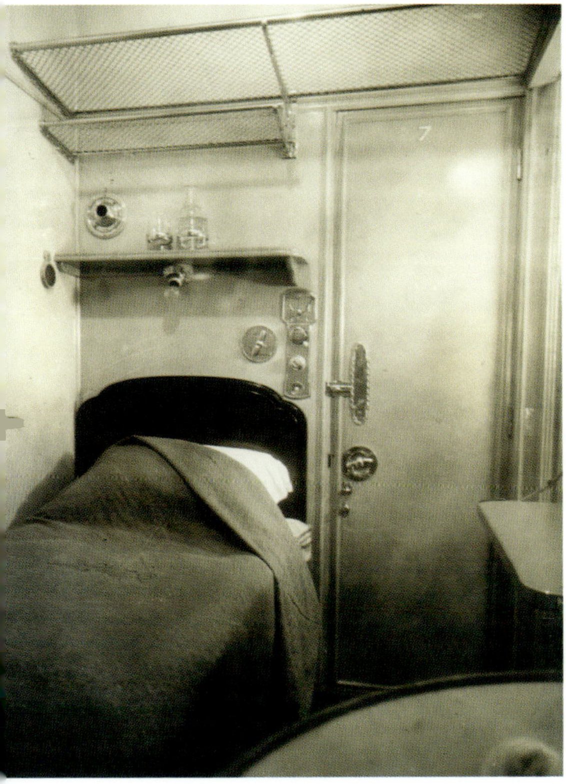

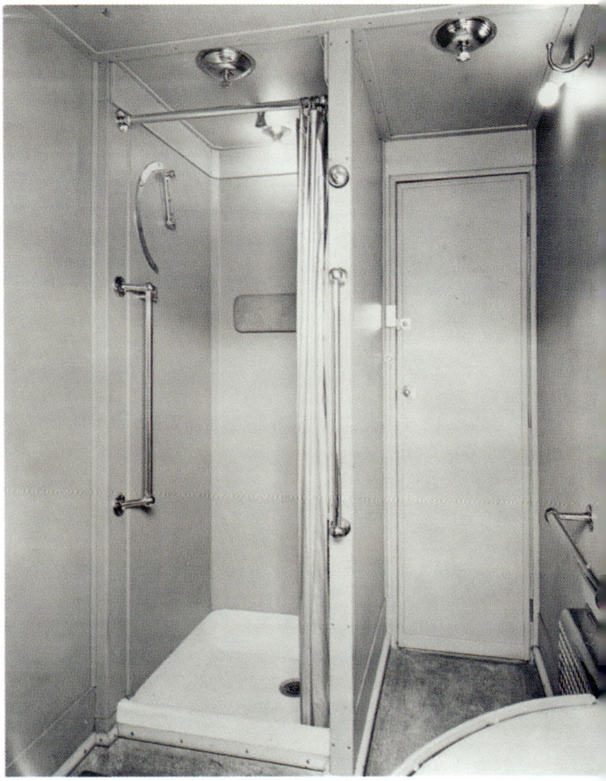

Above left: LNER first-class sleeping compartment, 1930s. (Author's collection)

Above right: LNER first-class shower compartment, 1930s. A civilized, but underused, facility! (Board of Trustees of the Science Museum)

On the LNER Sir Nigel Gresley installed a self-contained water heating system on a handsome 60-ft, eight-wheeler vehicle, while, not to be outdone, the LMS in 1933 introduced an up-to-date sleeping carriage, with walnut- and sycamore-lined corridors and thick patterned carpets, designed by William Stanier, on a twelve-berth, 69-ft body length.

The LMS named its premier service to Scotland the Royal Highlander in 1927, leaving Euston at 7.30 p.m. and arriving at Perth at 5.24 a.m. the following morning, where a breakfast car was attached for the run to Inverness. This was a heavy train, consisting of twelve to fourteen carriages, including a restaurant car, and often pulled by double-headed Stanier Class 5 4-6-0 locomotives to cope with the formidable climb from Blair Atholl to Druimuachdar Summit, 1,484 ft above sea level, and from Aviemore to Slochd Summit, 1,350 ft above the sea. In the same year another named train, the Aberdonian, ran up the East Coast, with sleeping cars for Fort William being split off at Edinburgh. The train was pulled by a 4-6-0 Pacific locomotive as far as Edinburgh, and then a Class P2 2-8-2 designed by Sir Nigel Gresley, for the difficult run to Aberdeen. These trains feature prominently in some of the murder/mystery stories of the time, notably in *The Singing Sands* by Josephine Tey, who lived in Inverness and regularly travelled on the Royal Highlander when she visited London.

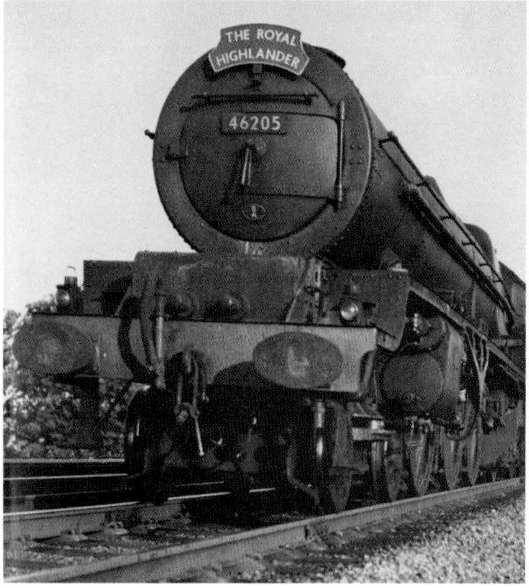

The Royal Highlander headed by *Princess Victoria* 46205 near Watford on its first run after the end of the Second World War. (Author's collection)

There is a splendidly atmospheric account of the final part of the journey on the Highland Line to Inverness in *Romantic Railways* by Kenneth Westcott Jones, published in 1971:

> As the *Royal Highlander* pulls away from Aviemore at 7.21 a.m., the restaurant car is busy with breakfast on this last stretch, with an hour left in which to provide bacon and eggs or Scots kippers, scones and other trimmings of the first Scottish meal taken amid some of the finest scenery in the Highlands. There is one more climb to make, the steepest of all but comparatively short as the direct line to Inverness is lifted over Slochd Summit. For three miles the gradient is 1 in 60, and speed falls to under twenty-five miles an hour. Once over the top the view opens out to the glorious 'Laigh O'Moray' country beside the sparkling Firth lying several hundred feet below the train. In between lies Culloden Moor which the train crosses, running through Culloden station five miles before Inverness. Close by are the graves of the Highlanders who were killed here in 1746, in the last major battle to be fought on British soil.
>
> Mere minutes later the grey dignified buildings of the Highland capital are closing in on the line and the high hills beside the River Ness make a pleasing setting. The train stops and reverses into the small terminal station, coming to rest 568 miles from London alongside a shorter train which stands ready to leave for Wick and Thurso with some of the mail and passengers brought by the *Royal Highlander*.

After the Second World War and the nationalisation of the railways in 1948, sleeping cars continued to run to over thirty destinations in England and Scotland, with new Mark I carriages introduced in 1957, then Mark 3 air-conditioned carriages in the 1980s, and most recently Mark 5 carriages with full en suite facilities which were brought into service in 2018, branded as Caledonian Sleeper and now managed by the Scottish government.

Many people have vivid memories of travelling on these overnight trains in the post-war years, and their accounts feature in my book *Anglo-Scottish Sleepers* (Amberley Publishing,

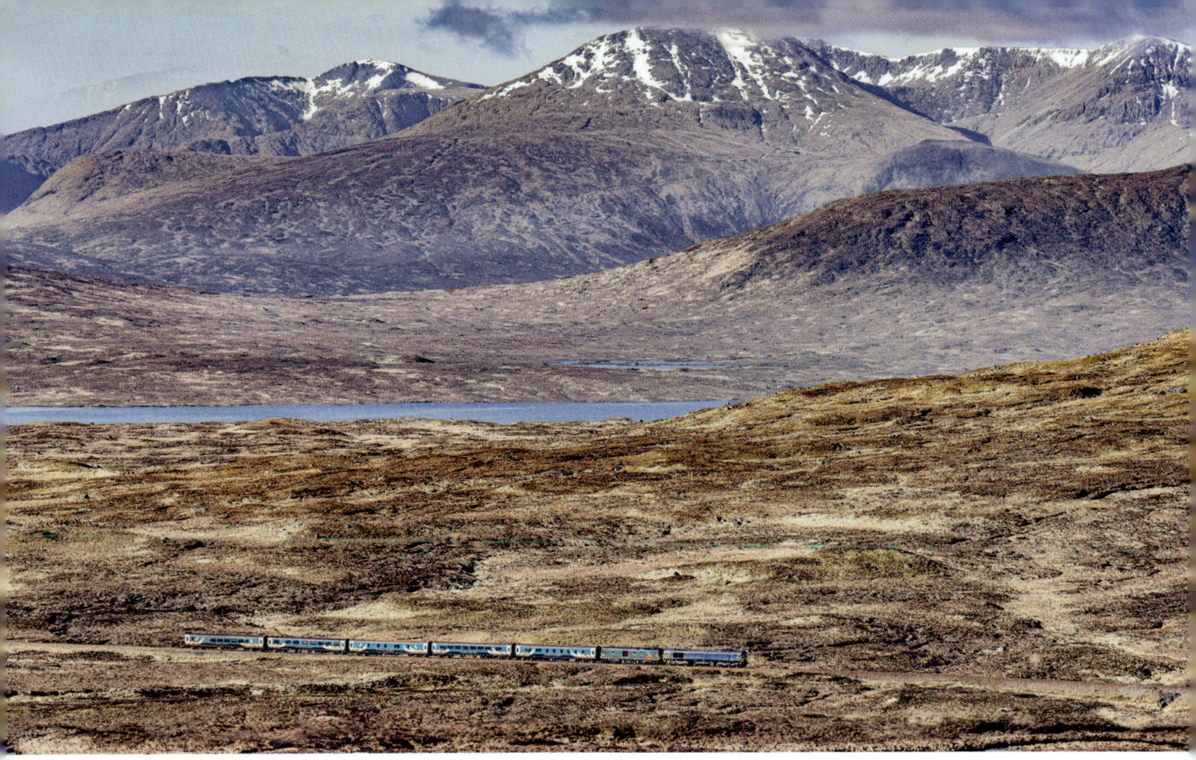

The Caledonian Sleeper with the new Mark 5 rolling stock near Gorton on the West Highland Line to Fort William. (Norman McNab)

2018). With the end of the Steam Age some of the romance of overnight travel died out, but the Caledonian Sleeper still provides an unrivalled sense of excitement, anticipation and a bit of mystery on its journeys between London and the Highlands of Scotland.

The travel writer Paul Theroux, who once disparagingly described a sleeper cabin as 'a cupboard with forward movement', nevertheless wrote lyrically about night trains in his book *The Great Railway Bazaar*:

> The romance associated with the sleeping car derives from its extreme privacy. Whatever drama is being enacted in this moving bedroom is heightened by the landscape passing the window: a swell of hills, the surprise of mountains, the loud metal bridge, or the melancholy sight of people standing under yellow lamps. And the notion of travel as a continuous vision, a grand tour's succession of memorable images across a curved earth – with none of the distorting emptiness of air or sea – is possible only on a train. A train is a vehicle that allows residence: dinner in the diner, nothing could be finer.

As we have seen, such a promising environment couldn't help but lend itself to becoming the setting for fictional stories of dastardly deeds on the railway, and occasionally sleeper trains feature in these. Canon Victor Whitechurch became known for his detective stories collected together in *Thrilling Stories of the Railway*, published in 1912. One of them entitled *A Perilous Ride* is narrated by 'Koravitch', who received a message from a secret society to which he belonged: 'Use every effort to prevent *Scotch Express* 8 p.m. from Newston to-morrow

(Thursday) arriving at Aberdeen before *Great East Northern* train. Most important. See papers.' The plot concerns an Austrian diplomatic envoy trying to get to Balmoral before the British prime minister to influence the queen about 'the Bulgarian Question'. This occurs at the time of The Race to the North in 1895, as Whitechurch explains in an extract from a daily paper:

> THE RACE TO THE NORTH
> Yesterday morning the *West Northern Express* was again to the front in the railway race, arriving at Aberdeen at 5.15 a.m., while its rival from Queen's Cross reached that station at 5.31. Last night both trains started at 8 o'clock, the drivers keenly alive to the work required of them, but, of course, we go to press too early to know the result of their respective journeys. To-night, however, it is anticipated that the race will be more exciting than ever, for the West Northern officials state that they will not only run the express in two portions, but that the first half will only consist of four coaches, and they are pretty well determined that it will not only beat their rival, but also prove a record run. Those who favour the Great East Northern Route will also be interested to hear that every possible pains are being taken in order that to-night's run shall also be a record.

In spite of Koravitch succeeding in delaying the West Northern Sleeping Car Express, there is a twist at the end of the story related to bets placed on The Race to the North. The story ends with Whitechurch giving a note of the actual times of arrival at Aberdeen of the rival trains in August 1895:

	West Coast	**East Coast**
August 20th	4.58 a.m.	5.11 a.m.
August 21st	4.51 a.m.	4.40 a.m.
August 22nd	4.32 a.m.	6.23 a.m.

Another writer who was meticulous in his railway details and intricate plotting was the Irish writer Freeman Wills Crofts (1879–1957). Crofts was born in Dublin, but the

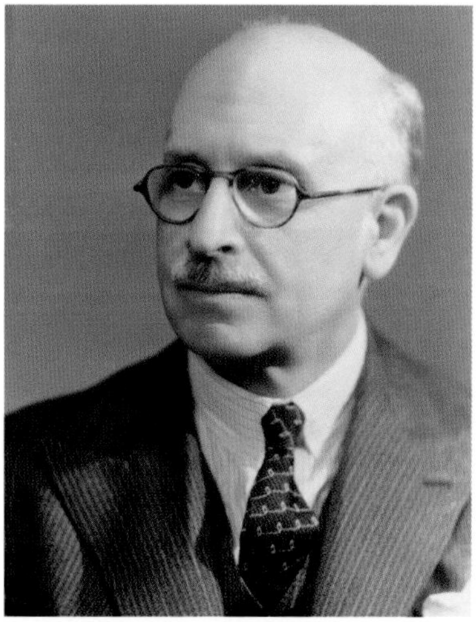

Freeman Wills Crofts (1879–1957).
(National Portrait Gallery)

family soon moved to Belfast where he became a pupil civil engineer on the Belfast & Northern Counties Railway. During a period of illness in 1912 he began writing his first detective story, eventually published as *The Cask* in 1920. Described by Dorothy Sayers as 'our cunningest fitter of jigsaws', he created his fictional detective Joseph French, whose painstaking methods feature in over thirty novels and numerous short stories.

Crofts was influenced both by the Sherlock Holmes stories and the novels of R. Austin Freeman and his detective Dr John Thorndyke. Crofts always worked out his plots in advance, putting together a detailed synopsis and chronology of the main incidents before he began writing the novel. In one of his short stories, *The Mystery of the Sleeping Car Express*, written in 1921 and published in 1956 but set in 1909 on the 10.30 p.m. North Western Railway Sleeping Car Express from London Euston, a man and a woman are found murdered between Preston and Carlisle. Crofts set the scene:

> It was generally a heavy train ... and two engines hauled behind them eight large sleeping cars, two firsts, two thirds, and two vans, half of which went to Glasgow, and the remainder to Edinburgh. It is essential to the understanding of what follows that the composition of the rear portion of the train should be remembered.

Crofts helpfully provides a diagram of the configuration of the train, and the mystery of how the couple were killed is unravelled by Inspector French, aided by a death-bed confession.

Crofts also wrote a full-length novel about a murder on an overnight sleeper to Stranraer, *Sir John Magill's Last Journey*. When he wrote it in 1930 the Northern Irishman left Euston at 7.10 p.m. for Stranraer, using the now-defunct line from Dumfries via Newton Stewart, and connecting with the boat to Larne in Northern Ireland. The plot concerns Sir John Magill, an Irish linen millionaire, who takes the sleeper to Stranraer and the boat to Larne and then disappears, his body eventually discovered in a shallow grave on the edge of his son's estate. Inspector French's investigations focus on a cruise taken by Sir John's nephew, and on the train journey from Euston. It was Crofts' favourite novel and was

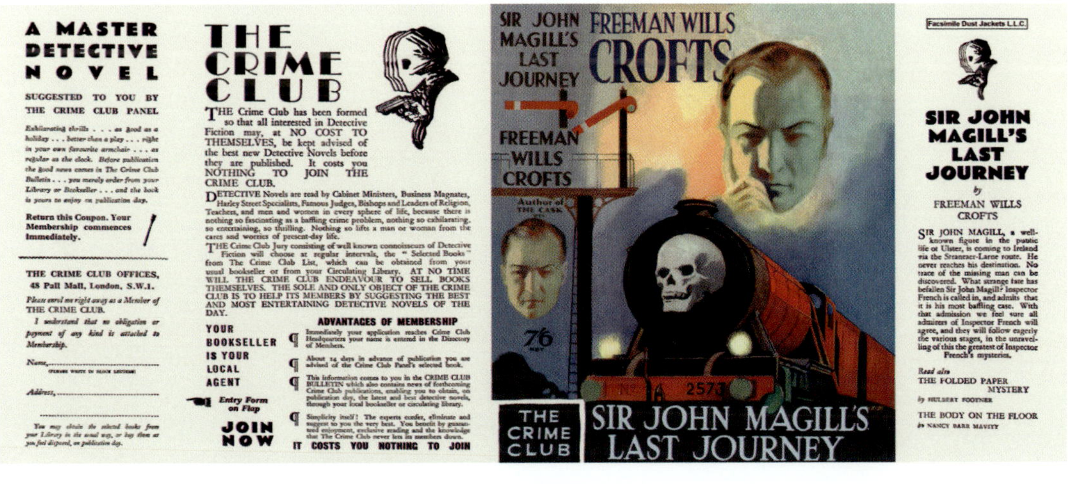

Book cover of Freeman Wills Crofts' *Sir John Magill's Last Journey*, first edition, William Collins & Sons Ltd, 1930. (Facsimile Dust Jackets L. L. C.)

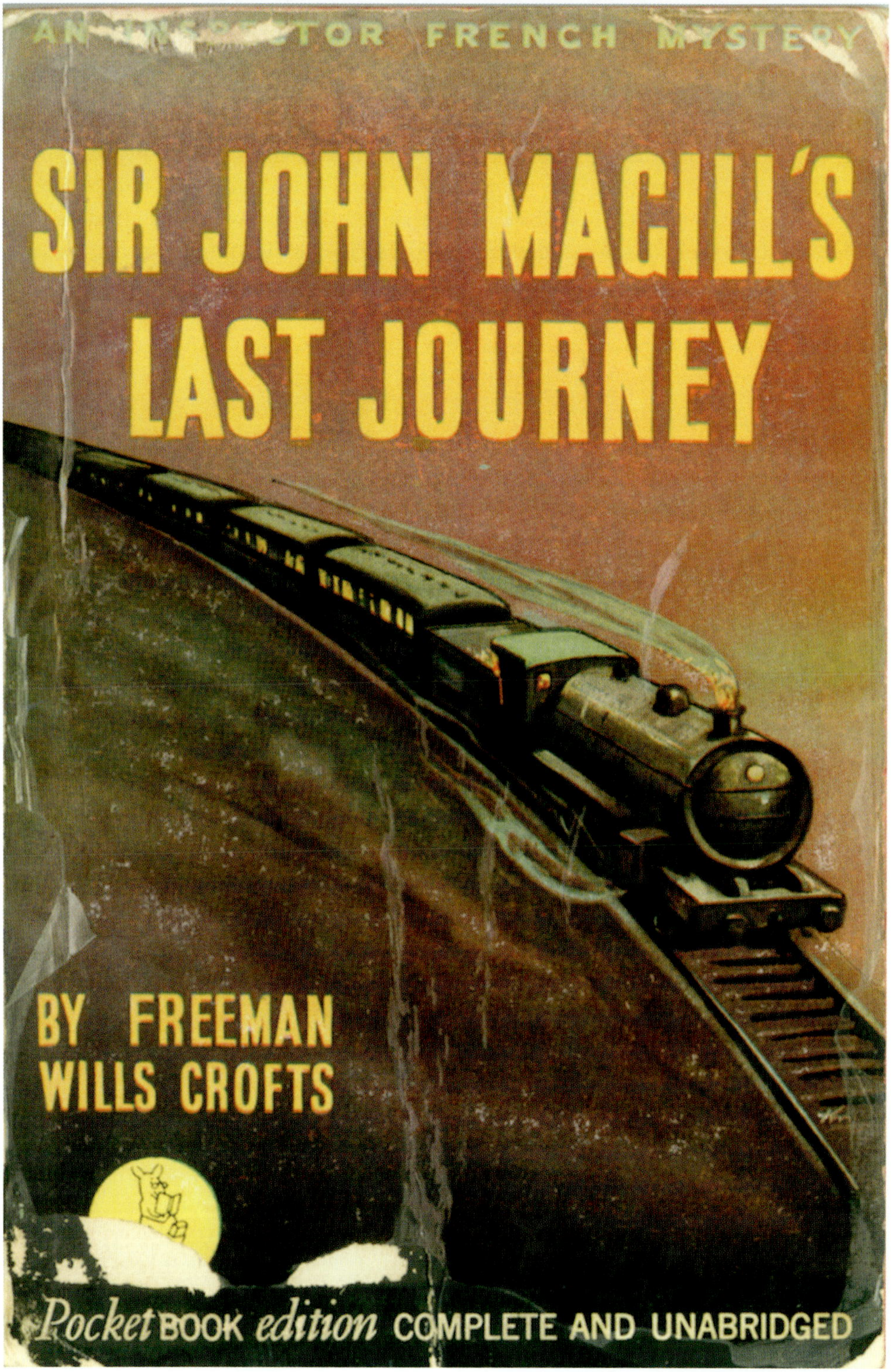

Book cover of Freeman Wills Crofts' *Sir John Magill's Last Journey*, paperback edition, Pocket Books, 1941. (Author's collection)

perhaps the most ingenious alibi plot he wrote, revolving around the intricate details of railway timetables and the complicated itinerary of a motor launch. In the novel French travels frequently between London and Stranraer on the sleeper. Croft even manages to weave in the Cornish Riviera Express and the Night Riviera from Plymouth to arrange for Inspector French to fall into conversation with his suspects, thus setting them up for the final denouement.

Another Golden Age writer who frequently used sleeper trains was Josephine Tey, the nom de plume of Elizabeth MacKintosh (1896–1952), who lived in Inverness, the daughter of a local fruit merchant. After her mother's death she kept house for her father and began her career as a writer. Her first mystery novel was *The Man in the Queue* (1925), in which Inspector Alan Grant of Scotland Yard makes his first appearance. Under the nom de plume of Gordon Daviot she also wrote a number of plays, including the historical drama *Richard of Bordeaux*, which ran for two years at the Arts Theatre in London (1932–33), starring John Gielgud. She knew many in the London literary and theatre world and travelled frequently between Inverness and London by the overnight sleeper.

Tey's final novel, *The Singing Sands* (1952), published after her death, begins with the discovery of a body in a berth on the sleeper. Inspector Grant, who is also on the train, takes the dead man's newspaper and discovers a short poem, 'The Singing Sands', written in a margin. He follows up the dead man's trail, which takes him to the Western Isles and an encounter with Scottish Nationalists, ranging far and wide before ending in London.

It was the most autobiographical of all Tey's novels, beginning with a description of the train journey north to what must surely be Inverness station:

> It was six o'clock of a March morning, and still dark. The long train came sidling through the scattered lights of the yard, clicking gently over the points. Into the glow of the signal cabin and out again. Under the solitary emerald among the rubies on the signal bridge. On towards the empty grey waste of platform that waited under the arcs. The *London Mail* at the end of its journey.

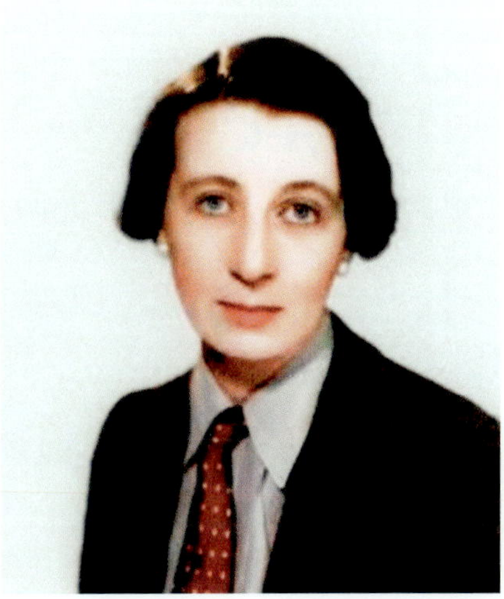

Josephine Tey (1896–1952).

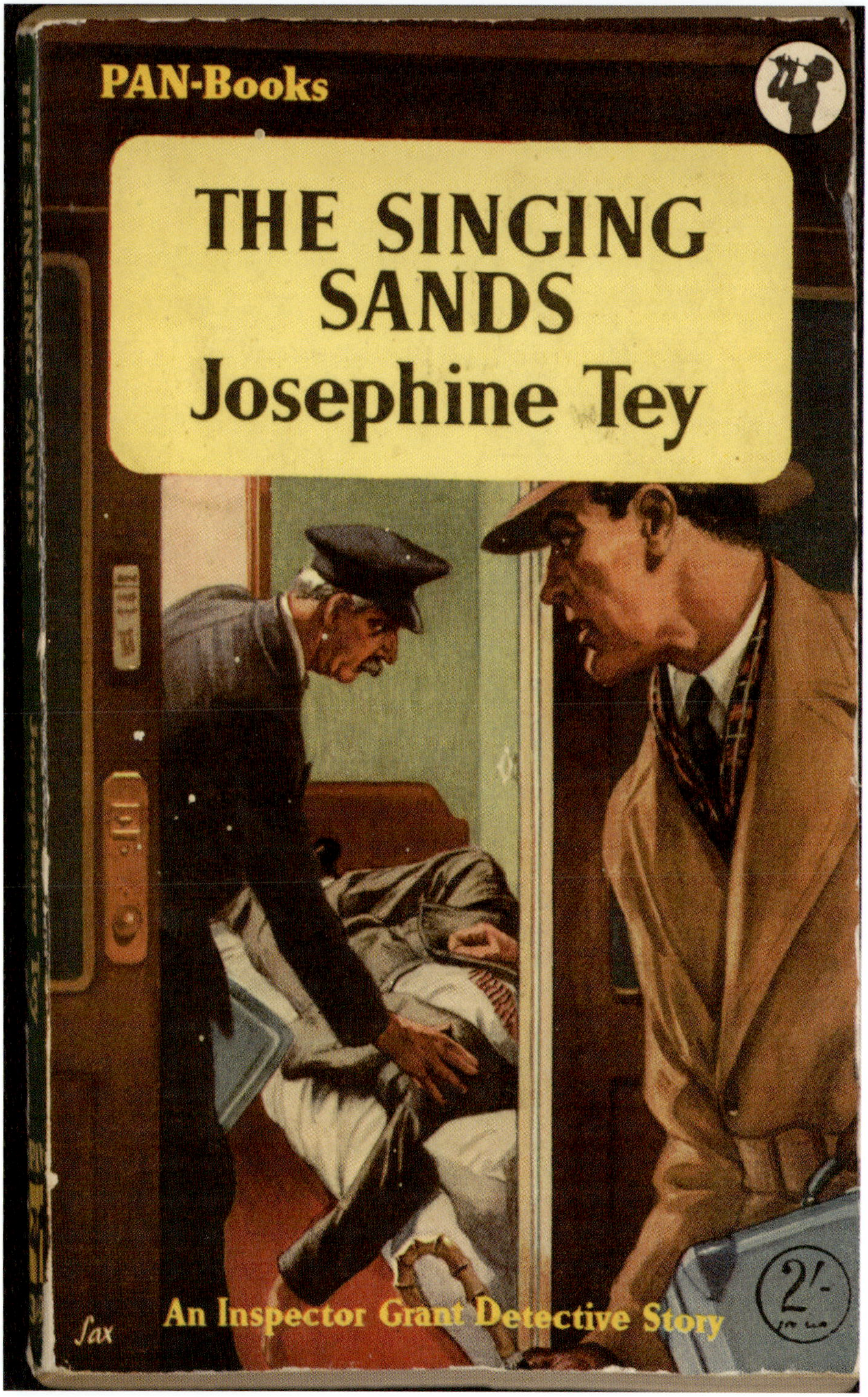

Book cover of Josephine Tey's *The Singing Sands*, 1952. The cover depicts the discovery by the sleeping car attendant and Inspector Grant of a dead body in one of the compartments. (Author's collection)

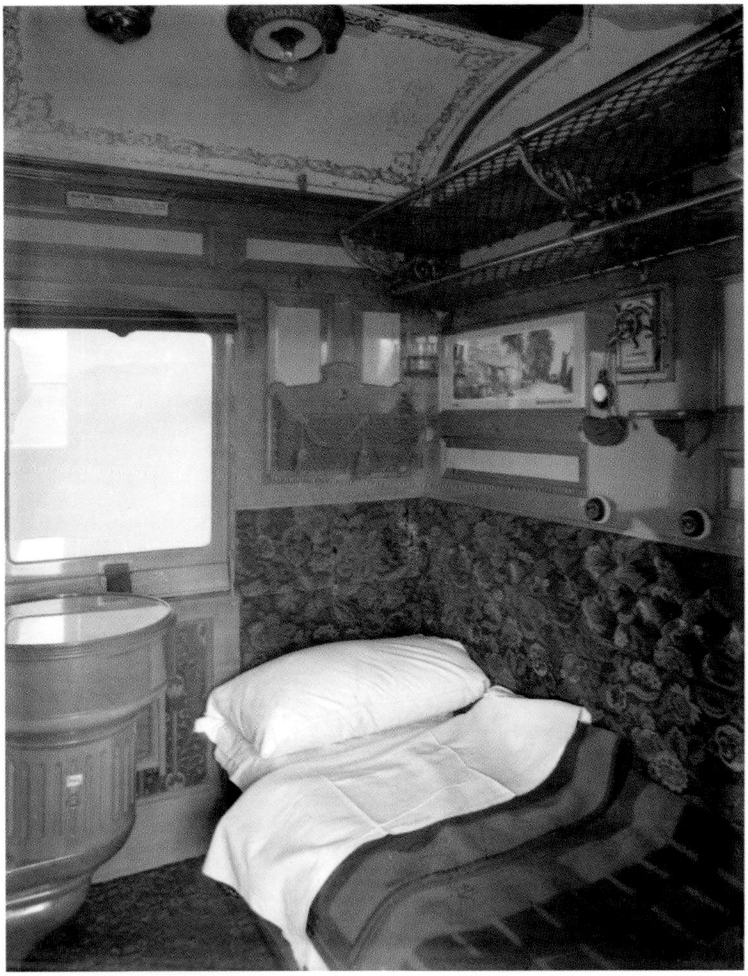

Interior of Midland Railway sleeping compartment carriage No. 2778, showing the bed made up and the corner washstand, 1920, just as Josephine Tey describes it in *The Singing Sands*. (Board of Trustees of the Science Museum)

Tey then gives a wonderfully accurate description of a sleeping berth:

> The compartment represented A Small Enclosed Space. To the normal eye the compartment was just a neat little room with a bunk, a wash-basin, a mirror, luggage racks in assorted sizes, shelves that appeared or disappeared as bidden, a fine little drawer for one's hypothetical valuables, and a hook for one's presumably unhocked watch.

Tey called the train the Flying Highlander, surely in reality the Royal Highlander, with its surly attendant Murdo Gallacher, and she bases some of the characters on members of her family. The book is nominally set in Perthshire, but the details suggest that Inverness was the real setting, from the moment Grant gets off the train and walks into the Station Hotel, right next to the station.

Contemporary Scottish crime writer Val McDermid has argued that Josephine Tey opened the door for later writers like Ruth Rendell to explore the darker side of humanity, and

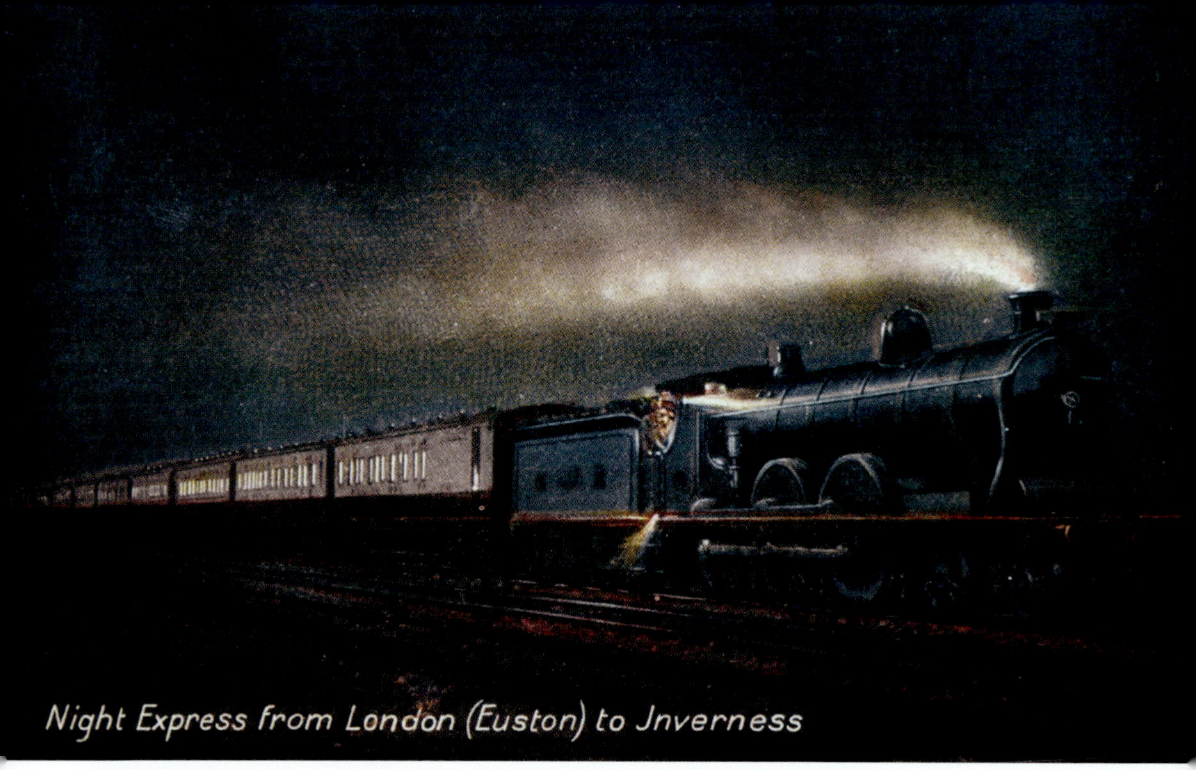

A colour print of the Night Express to Inverness via the West Coast route, hauled by a Caledonian 4-6-0 locomotive, 1903. (Board of Trustees of the Science Museum)

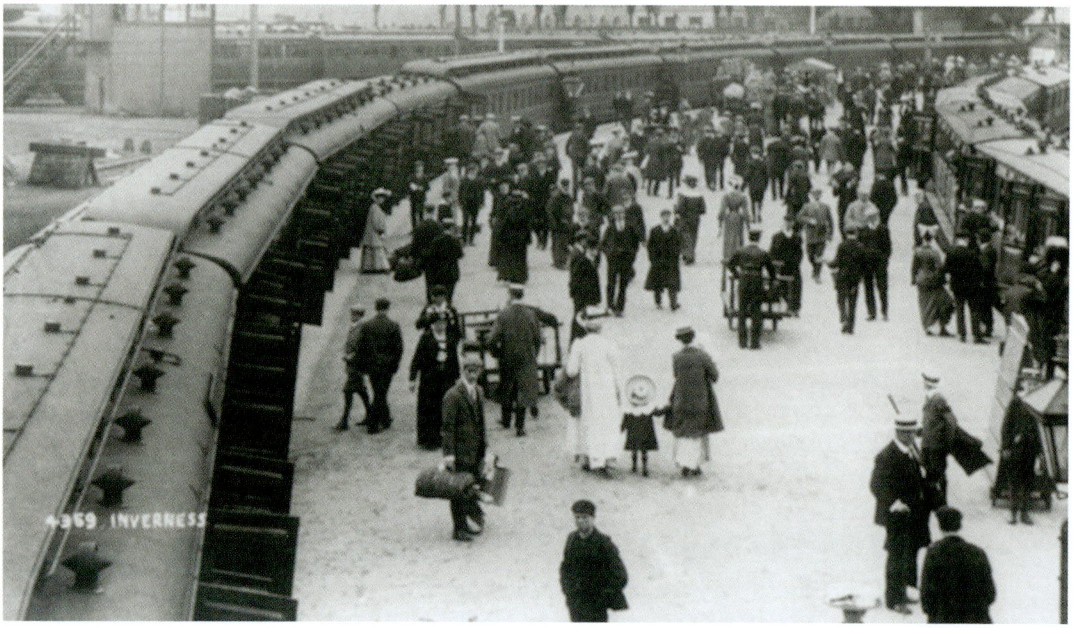

Inverness station with the London overnight sleeper at the platform, early twentieth century. (Author's collection)

created a bridge between the Golden Age of Detective Fiction and crime novels of the modern era.

As already noted, in the years after the demise of steam on the British railway network the number of crime novels involving sleeper trains sharply declines, but there are one or two exceptions. In Philip McCutchan's *Overnight Express* (1988) Arab terrorists seize control of a night train on the East Coast Main Line and threaten to blow it up on the Durham Viaduct unless three of their comrades are released from prison. Coincidentally, eleven Conservative Members of Parliament are on board, and their survival is deemed vital to ensure that the slim Conservative majority in the House of Commons is maintained. As Philip Scowcroft notes in his survey of the genre, all ends well for British Rail, the viaduct and the government!

In the twenty-first century, however, interest in the sleeper as a setting for murder/mystery novels is enjoying a revival, interestingly the first being a series of stories for children, all set on trains, and beginning with *Highland Falcon Thief*, by M. G. Leonard and Sam Sedgman, with lovely illustrations by Elisa Paganelli, published in 2020. Harrison Beck and his Uncle Nat are enjoying the final journey of the Highland Falcon, Britain's most famous royal steam train. When a precious jewel goes missing, Harrison and his friend Lenny find themselves at the centre of the investigation and decide to solve the mystery before the journey ends. It is an Agatha Christie-style whodunnit, with lots of steam train detail, and captures very effectively the romance of the railways. The other titles in the series are: *Kidnap on the California Comet, Murder on the Safari Star, Danger at Dead Man's Pass, Sabotage on the Solar Express* and *The Arctic Railway Assassin.*

Alexandra Benedict's *Murder on the Christmas Express*, published in 2022, and subtitled *Eighteen passengers, seven stops, one killer*, is set on the present-day Caledonian Sleeper in the new Mark 5 carriages, although the endpaper carriage diagram in the book takes considerable artistic licence with their actual design. The diagram helpfully shows the distribution of Standard and Club cabins and marks the positions of each individual in the story. The train is the 21.15 p.m. Caledonian Sleeper service to Fort William, which gets hit by a snowstorm on Rannoch Moor and derailed.

The story opens with a murder in one of the cabins before introducing the cast of characters, including Roz Parker, a former detective in the Metropolitan Police, who is on her way to be with her daughter who is in labour. There is also a quiz team, Meg, a media influencer, a reality TV star, a stowaway and a dysfunctional family. Although it seems to be a cosy Agatha Christie-style Christmas mystery, in fact the novel deals with dark and serious issues including rape, coercive control and domestic violence. Although it is well written, it is tonally confused, an awkward mix of Golden Age and Crime Noir. It is also occasionally somewhat preachy and relies on significant evidence which is not revealed to the reader and only unveiled in the final solution, thus breaking one of the cardinal rules of the Golden Age of Detective Fiction. It is, however, full of suspense, and Benedict endearingly includes a Christmas quiz and a recipe for 'Tablet', a fudge-like sweet made in Scotland, at the end of the book.

In September 2024 the BBC broadcast the blockbuster real-time thriller *Nightsleeper*, again set on a modern Caledonian Sleeper train travelling from Glasgow Central station to London Euston. Cyberterrorists seize control of the sleeper and are driving the train remotely, with just a handful of passengers remaining on board, including Joe, an off-duty police officer, who takes charge of the fight-back and is in phone contact with Abby, acting

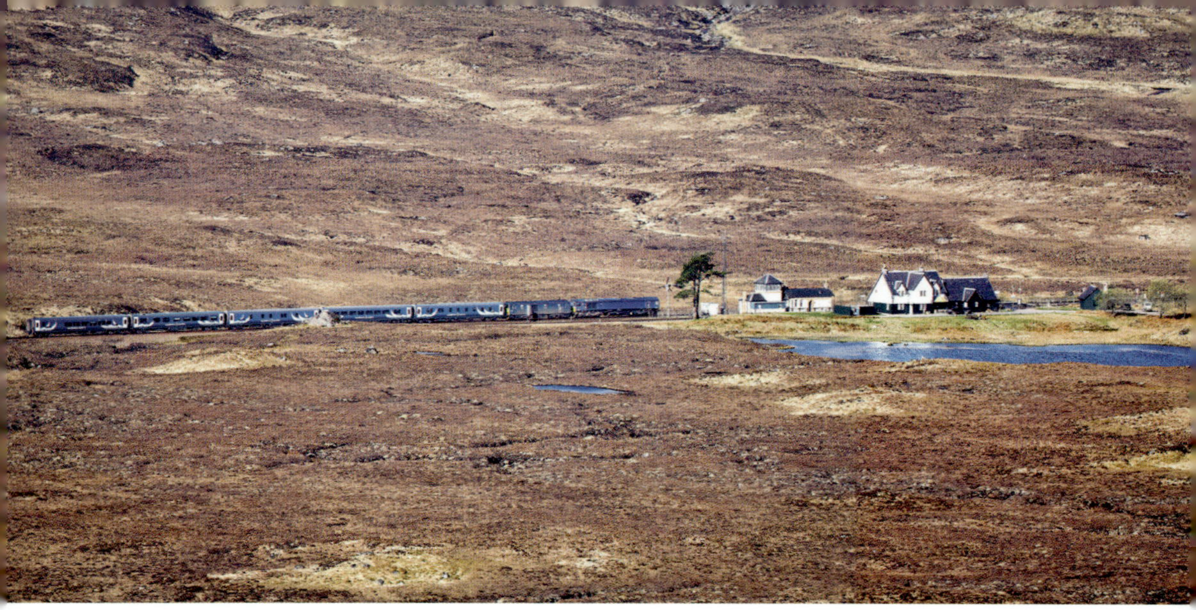

The Caledonian Sleeper at Corrour station, West Highland Line, Scotland, the place where the sleeper derailed in a snowdrift in Alexandra Benedict's novel *Murder on the Christmas Express*. (Norman McNab)

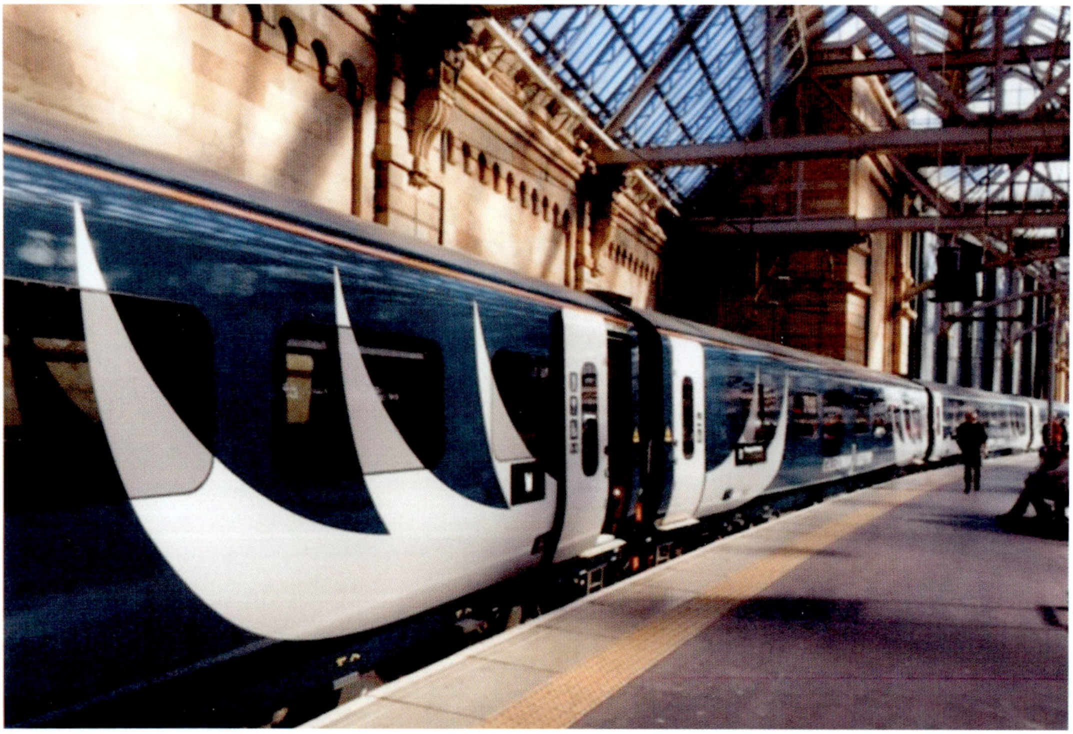

The *Caledonian Sleeper* at Glasgow Central station, 2019. This was the starting point for the BBC series *The Nightsleeper* in which cyberterrorists took control of an overnight sleeper train from Glasgow to London. (Author's collection)

technical director at the National Cyber Security Centre. Across six hour-long episodes, the time it would actually take the train to travel from Glasgow to London, they struggle to beat the clock and avoid a terrible disaster.

The script was written by Nick Leather, who had always wanted to write a locked-room mystery, and wove in his own experiences of travelling on the railway network. If you think the concept sounds implausible, it turns out that it could conceivably happen. Leather explains:

> We got three experts in a room to see if our premise was possible: an ethical hacker, a railway designer and a former government cyber expert who specialised in critical infrastructure. I feared they'd point out insurmountable obstacles and stop the idea in its tracks. In fact, within two hours, they said: 'Between us, we could do this. We could hack a train.'

The production team constructed a train simulator in a warehouse near Glasgow and filmed the route of the train which was then projected on LED screens outside the windows, so it looked realistic. Train and station announcements are realistically spoken by actual announcers, but because the system has been manipulated by the hacker, they say increasingly sinister things. Although the series was a success, Leather was asked if he thought it might put people off travelling on the Caledonian Sleeper, to which he replied: 'Look at Agatha Christie. Murder never did the Orient Express any harm, did it?'

3

The Continent of Europe: 'One is Just Killing Time on a Train'

In Vladimir Nabokov's novel *The Real Life of Sebastian Knight,* published in 1941, one character has:

> A strange, almost romantic passion for sleeping cars and Great European Express Trains ... the soft crackle of polished panels in the blue-shaded night, the long sad sigh of brakes at dimly surmised stations, the upward slide of an embossed leather blind disclosing a platform, a man wheeling luggage, the milky globe of a lamp with a pale moth whirling around it ....

Nabokov captures the mixture of luxury, anticipation and melancholy of night-time travel across Europe.

Although railways began in Britain, they soon spread to the Continent, where each nation approached railway development in different ways, spurred on by technological progress and the need for the rapid transport of military troops and equipment. However, by the same token, because of the fear of being invaded by a hostile power, each country had a strong desire to adopt an incompatible system and gauge to its neighbours to prevent enemy troops being brought in by rail. As in Britain, railways were initially built by private investors looking for quick profits. This resulted in no general standardised framework and railway companies

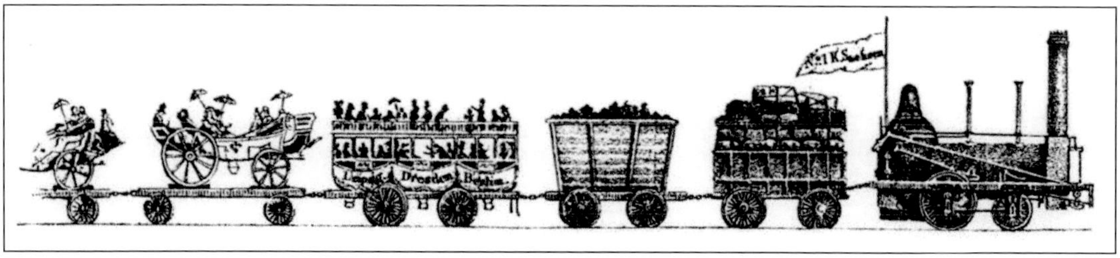

Print of an early steam train.

fortifying themselves within their own areas and national borders. However, governments soon began pressing for greater harmonisation and regulation of a European network that at one point boasted five different gauges and twenty-one different signalling systems.

Belgium took the lead in embracing the Industrial Revolution, and became a major contributor to early rail development, championing the creation of a national network. The first railway ran from Brussels to Mechelen and was completed in 1835. So, it is not surprising that it was a Belgian, Georges Nagelmackers (1845–1905), an engineer from Liége, who conceived the idea of creating a company to run luxurious railway carriages across Europe. In 1870 he published a proposal to develop sleeper carriages and in 1872 he founded the Compagnie Internationale des Wagons-Lits. He began by partnering with an American, Colonel William Mann, who invented the Mann Boudoir Car, but eventually

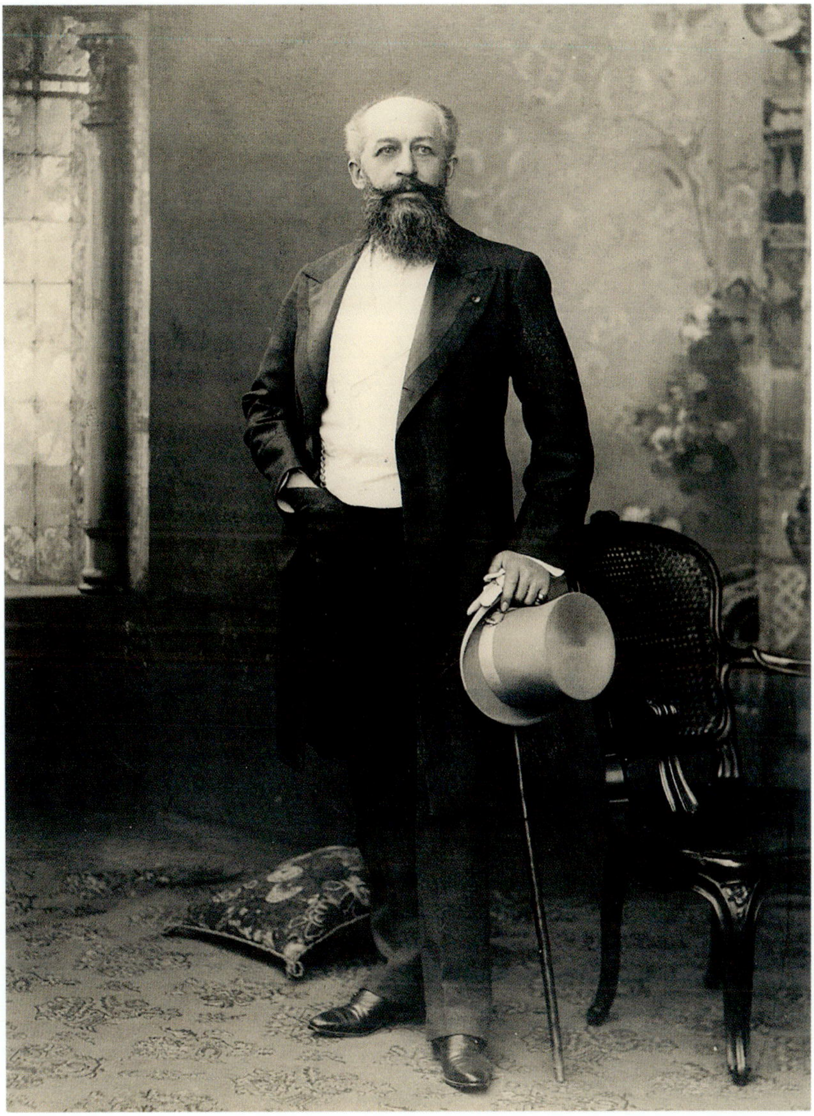

George Nagelmackers (1845–1905); portrait by Nadar. (CIWL archive (c Wagons-Lits Diffusion Phototeque))

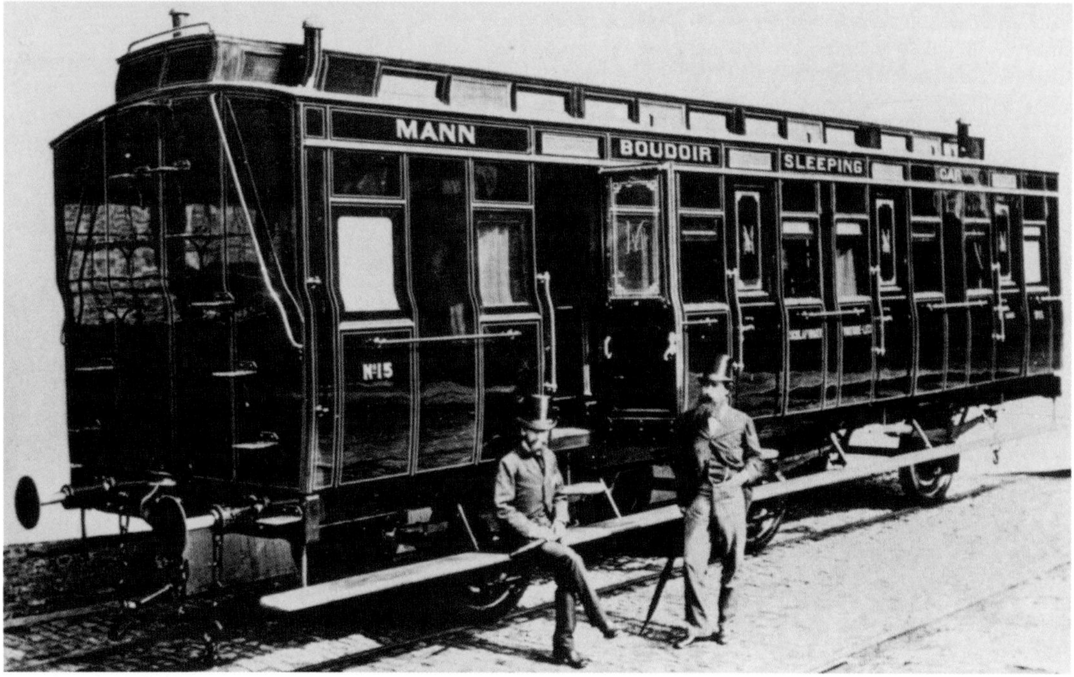

A Mann Boudoir Sleeping Car of 1873, with Colonel Mann seated on the running board and George Nagelmackers standing beside him.

bought him out in 1875. He ordered his first six-wheeler cars which were built in Vienna, and then another set of five built in Germany, and in May 1873 began running sleeping cars between Paris, Strasbourg and Vienna. His strategy was to convince train operators to attach his sleeping and restaurant cars to their trains, and to charge passengers a supplement for using them. Supported by King Leopold II of Belgium, who was an enthusiast for train travel, he formed a series of interlocking contracts on the Continent, built the first European bogie sleeping car and restaurant car in 1880, and in 1882 ran the first train composed solely of Wagons-Lits coaches between Paris Gare de l'Est and Vienna, in a time of twenty-eight hours. In 1883 he negotiated with eight railway companies for the Express d'Orient to run to Vienna, on to Romania and then by an eighteen-hour sea voyage to Constantinople. The Orient Express was born.

Pulled by an outside cylinder Est 2-4-0 locomotive, the varnished teak carriages were luxuriously appointed, with fine furnishings, plush carpets, washbasins and toilets. By 1889 the railway tracks were completed all the way through to Constantinople, the capital of the Ottoman Empire straddling the Bosphorus and the junction between Europe and the Orient. By 1905, when Nagelmackers died, he had had the satisfaction of seeing his Wagons-Lits established as an international brand serving various routes stretching across Europe and beyond.

The Simplon Tunnel was opened in 1905, and after the First World War the Simplon-Orient Express ran from Paris via Lausanne, Milan, Venice, Trieste, Zagreb, Belgrade, Nish and Sophia to Constantinople. During the 1920s the Wagons-Lits company built their most

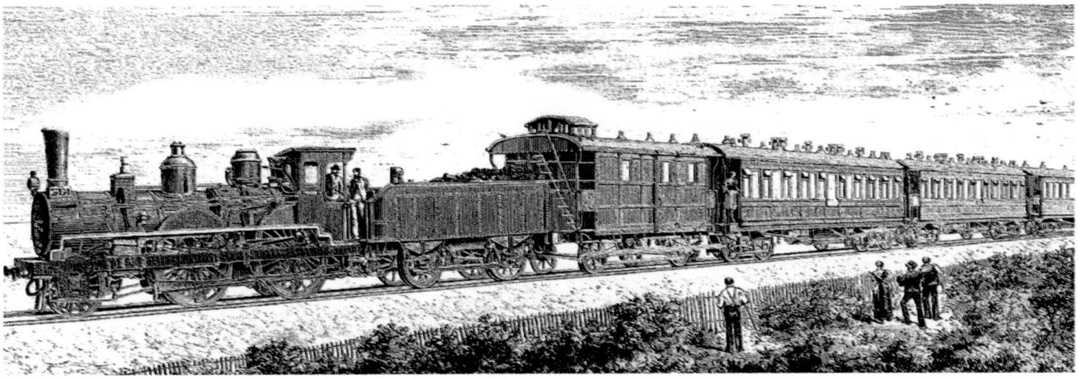

Illustration of the first train run by the Compagnie Internationale des Wagons-Lits, 1883. (CIWL archive (c Wagons-Lits Diffusion Phototeque))

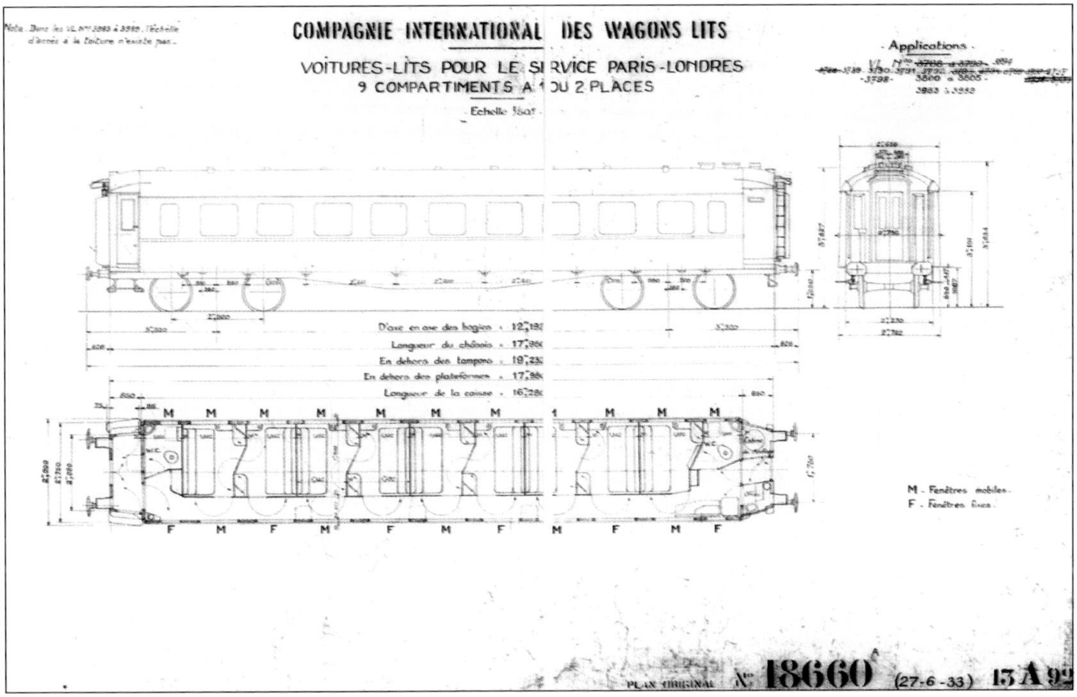

Engineering drawing of a Wagons-Lits carriage, 1933. (Board of Trustees of the Science Museum)

luxurious fleet of coaches, and these were used for the Orient Express and its variations, the Rome Express, the Nord Express to St Petersburg, the Sud-Express to Lisbon, the Blue Train to the French Riviera and the Night Ferry from London Victoria to Paris Gare du Nord.

After the Second World War many routes were curtailed as a consequence of the Communist Iron Curtain, and the service declined into a shadow of its former self, with

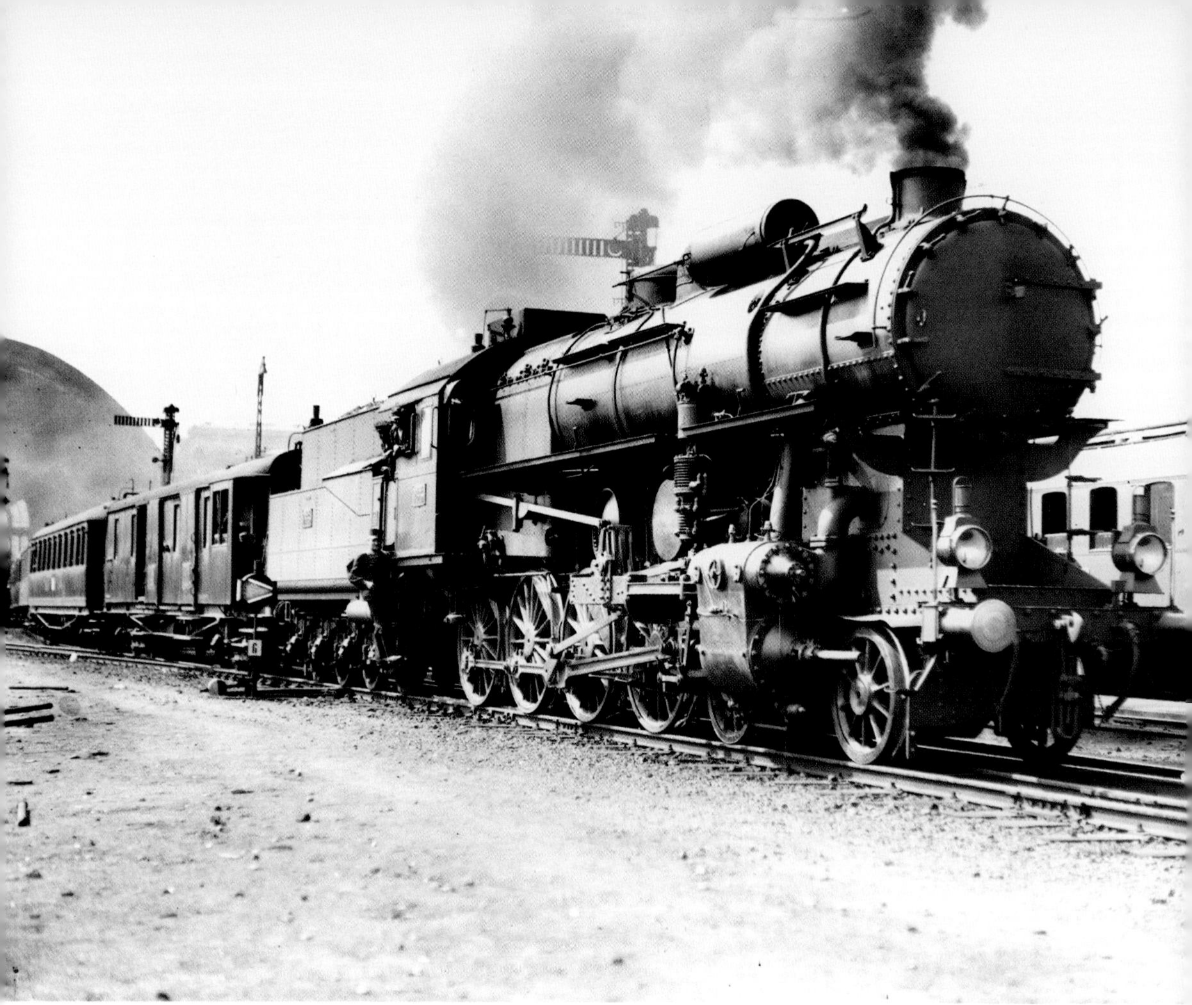

Steam-hauled MAV locomotive, Hungarian Railways, Class 4-8-0 No. 424. 010, leaving Budapest East station with the Simplon Orient Express, 1929. (Board of Trustees of the Science Museum)

often only a single sleeping car attached to a local train. In 1950 a two-man team from *LIFE Magazine*, reporter Roy Rowan and cameraman Jack Birns, set off on the Simplon Orient Express, starting at London Victoria, travelling to Paris and then on to Istanbul. The journey took eighty hours, and became much more spartan after they left Switzerland and proceeded eastwards through Yugoslavia, Bulgaria and into Turkey, with only seven first-class passengers left, including an American courier. Their resulting photographic account gives an accurate and atmospheric picture of the Orient Express in its twilight years. (For a full gallery of Jack Birns' photographs, see www.life.com>history<the-orient-express, and for a full account of his trip see retours.eu>01-simplon-orient-express.) The final run of the Orient Express left Paris on 19 May 1977 from the Gare de Lyon, with only one sleeping car and no restaurant car, and so the era of grand overnight European trains sadly came to an end.

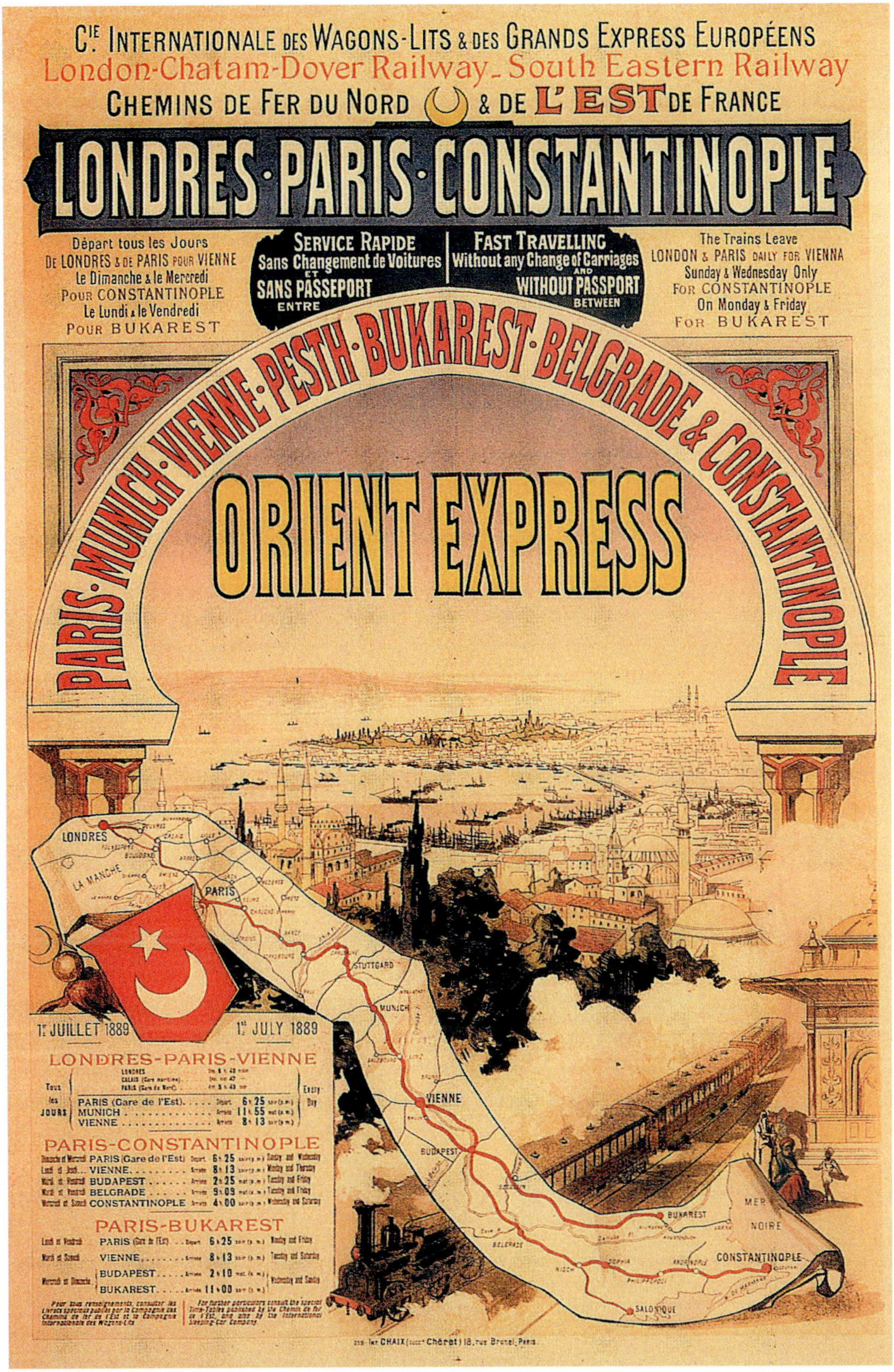

Poster for the 'Orient Express: Paris-Munich-Vienne-Budapest-Belgrade-Constantinople'. The design includes an image of the train, its route, a view of Constantinople and the Bosphorus, and the timetable for winter 1888–89. By Jules Cheret. (CIWL archive (c Wagons-Lits Diffusion Phototeque))

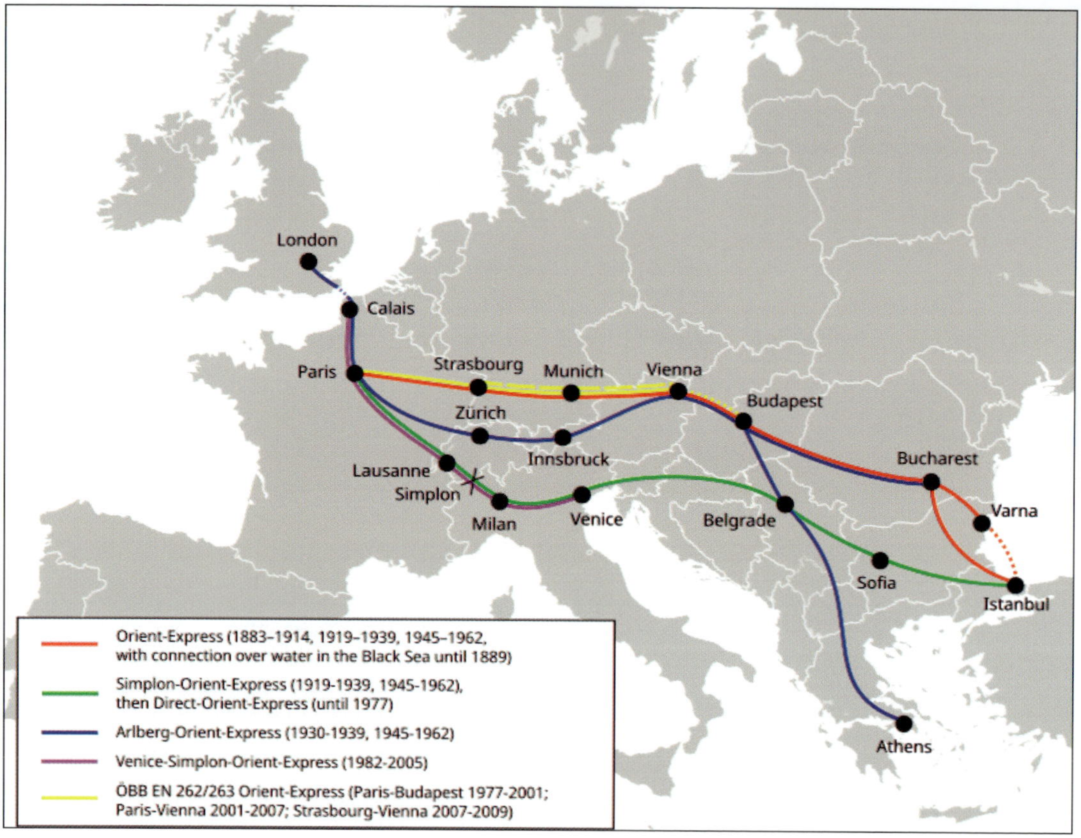

Map of the routes of the Orient Express. (Wikipedia Commons)

However, there was a lot of press coverage of the event, and as a result James Sherwood, the President of the Sea Containers Group, decided to try to recreate the train as it was in its luxury heyday. He bought two sleeping cars at auction, and they formed the nucleus of what became the Venice Simplon Orient Express (VSOE) launched in 1982. Sherwood began collecting and restoring all the sleeper, dining and Pullman carriages he could find, including Sleeping Car 3309, which had spent ten days stuck in a snowdrift in 1929, inspiring Agatha Christie to write *Murder on the Orient Express*. So, L'Express d'Orient lives on, albeit in luxury train mode and not as a regular daily service.

No other train has evoked so many murder plots, spy dramas and so much thrilling escapism as the Orient Express. It appears in more films, books and television plays than any other type of transport you could name. However, other Continental expresses also appear in fiction, the earliest of which is *The Rome Express* by Arthur George Frederick Griffiths, 1838–1908). Griffiths was a British military officer and author, who was born at Poona in India and served in the Crimean War, participating in the Siege of Sevastopol. He wrote extensively about prison life and also several mystery crime novels, including *The Passenger from Calais* (1906), which was based on a journey he made on the Engadine Express from Calais to Basle in July 1902.

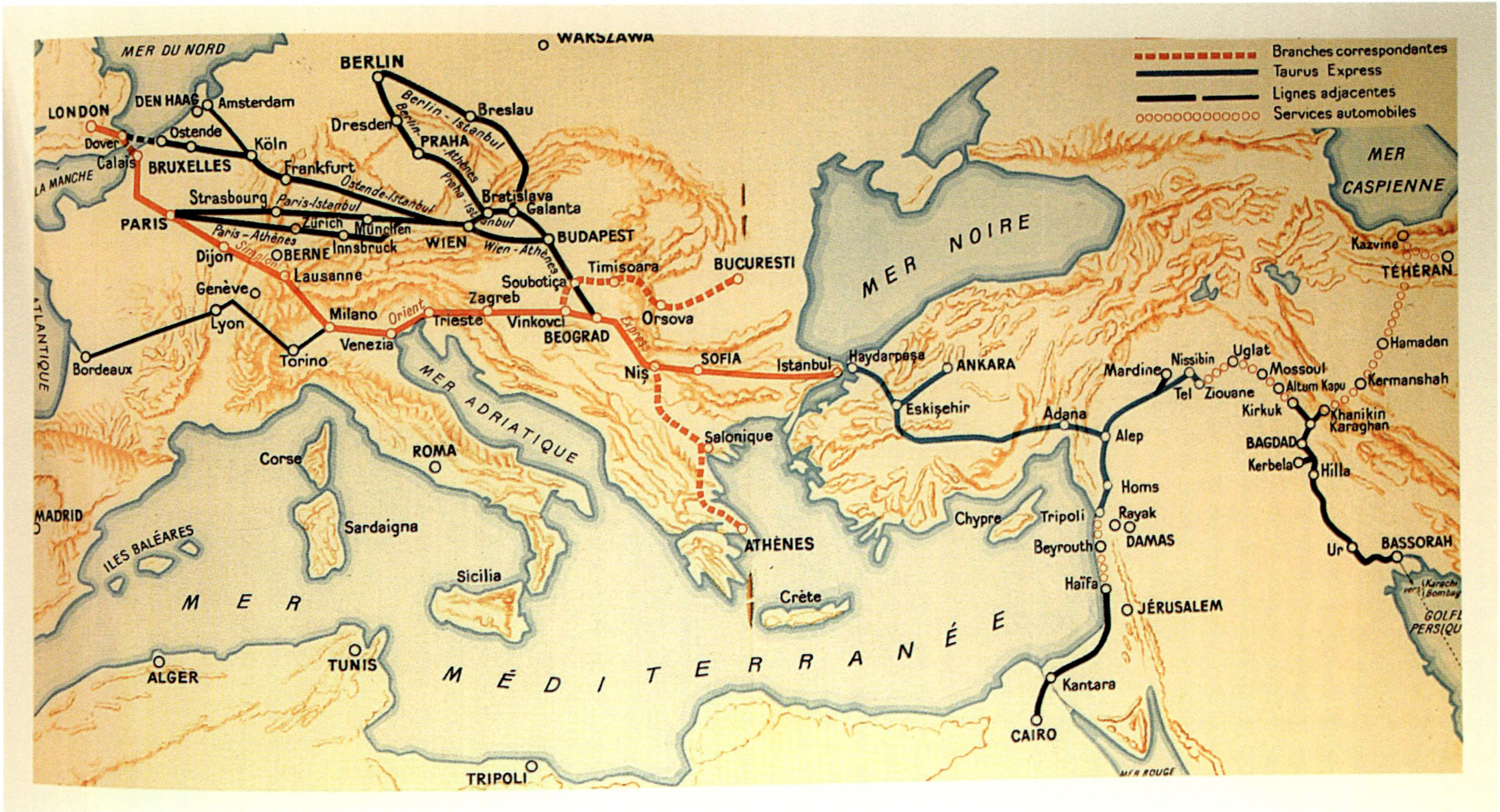

Map of the routes of the Simplon Orient/Taurus Express, published by the Wagons-Lits Company for 1930–31. (CIWL archive (c Wagons-Lits Diffusion Phototeque))

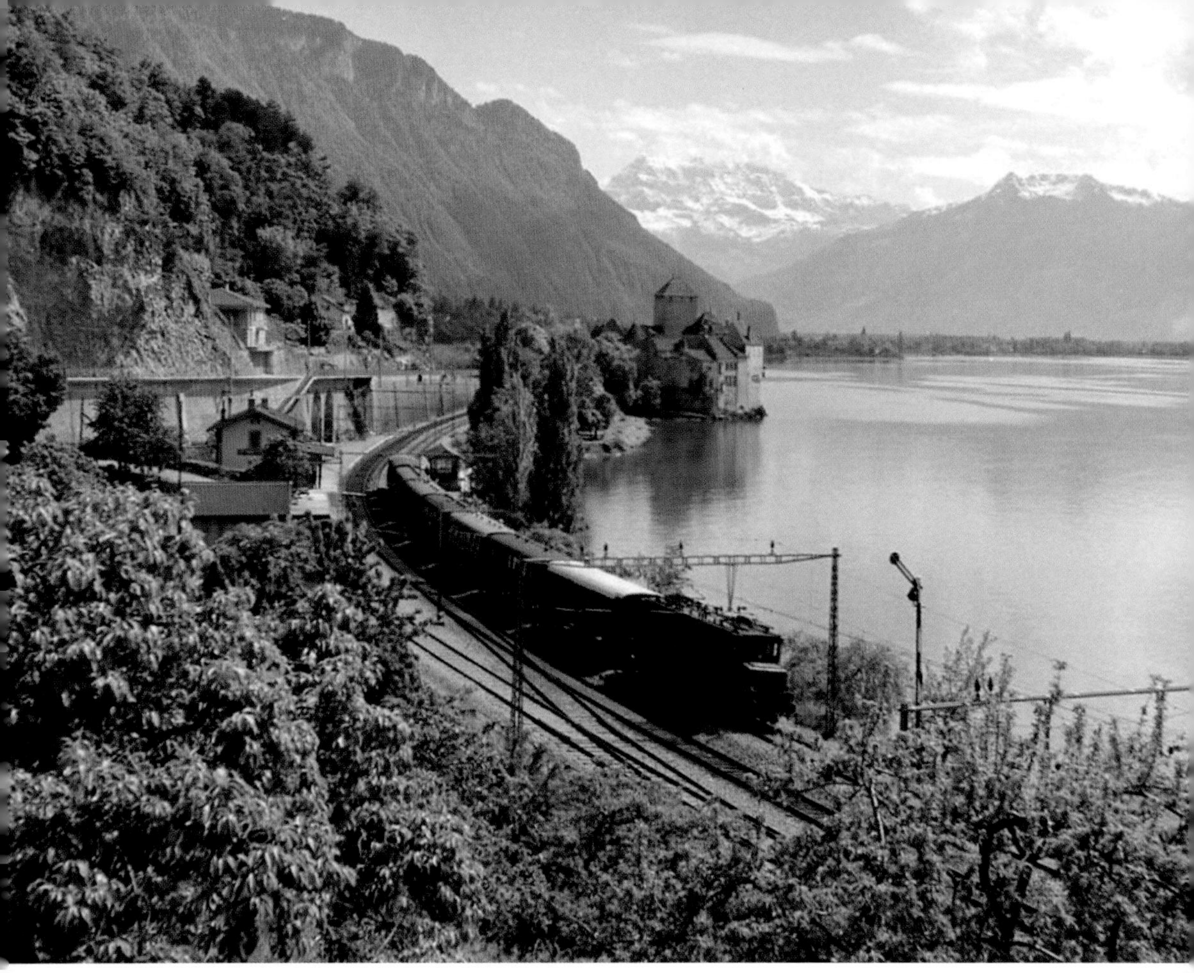

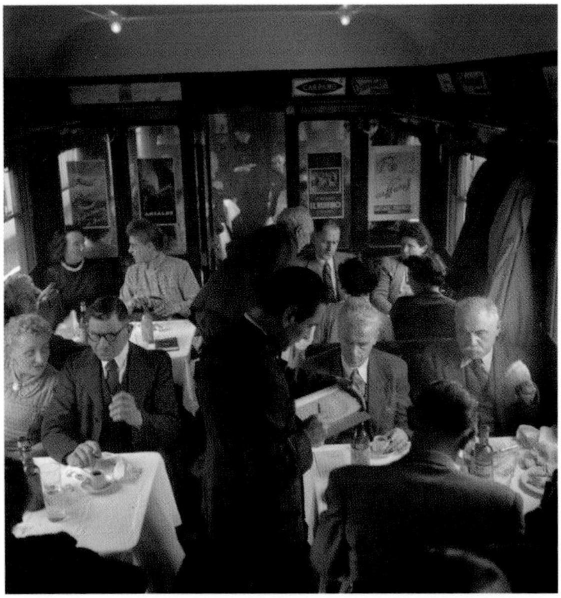

Above: The Simplon Orient Express travelling by the shores of Lake Geneva, Switzerland, 1950. By Jack Birns. (Shutterstock/ *Life* Jack Birns)

Left: In the restaurant car, Simplon Orient Express, 1950. By Jack Birns. (Shutterstock/ *Life* Jack Birns)

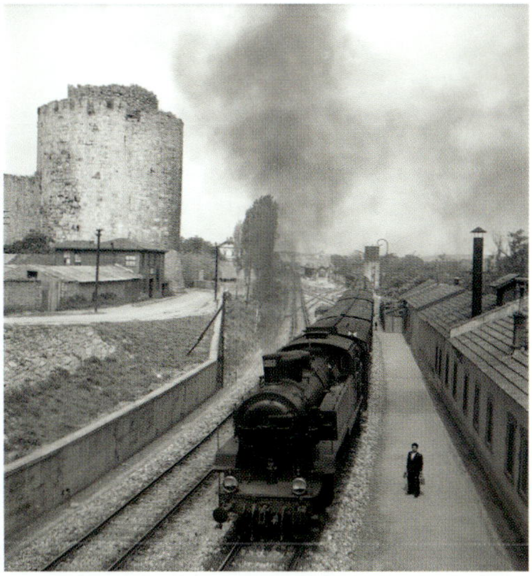

Right: The Simplon Orient Express approaching Istanbul, 1950. By Jack Birns. (Shutterstock/*Life* Jack Birns)

Below: An American courier being handed a diplomatic bag on the Simplon Orient Express, 1950. (CIWL archive (c Wagons-Lits Diffusion Phototeque))

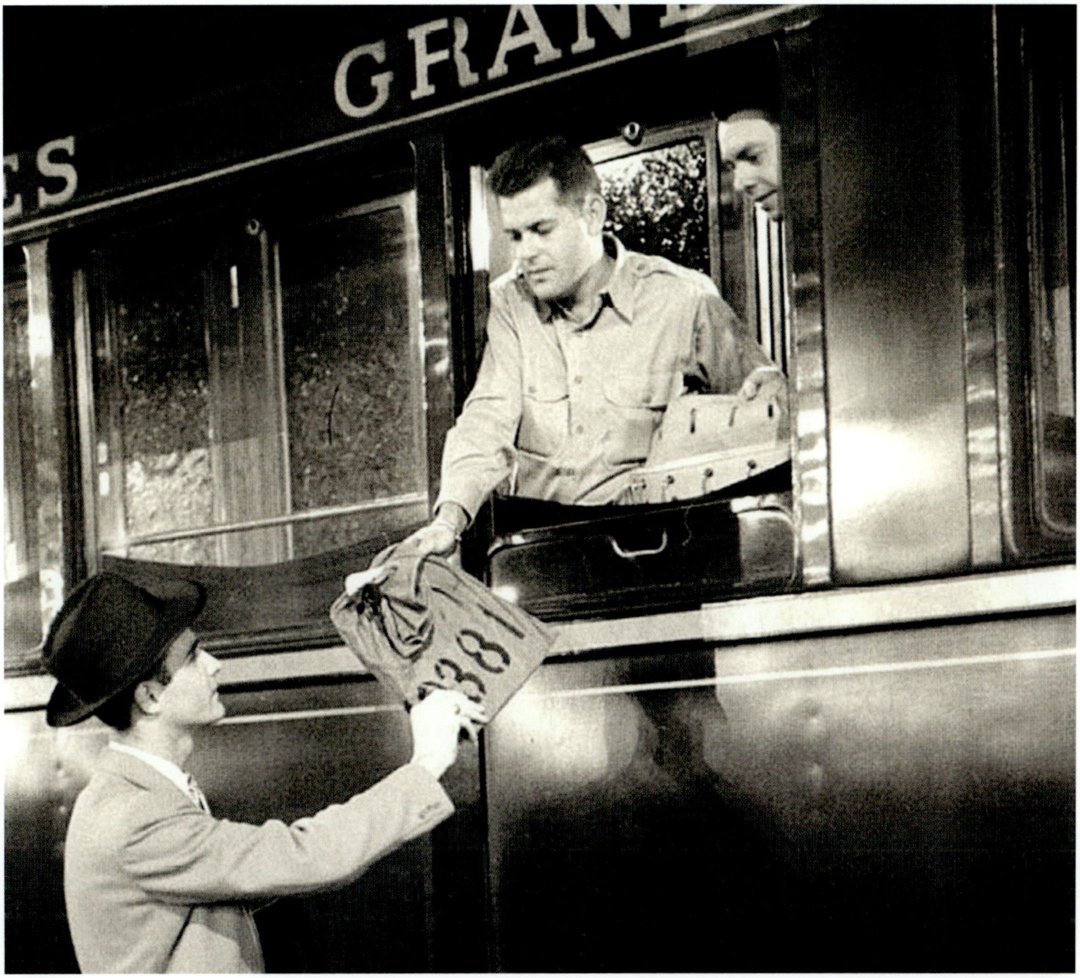

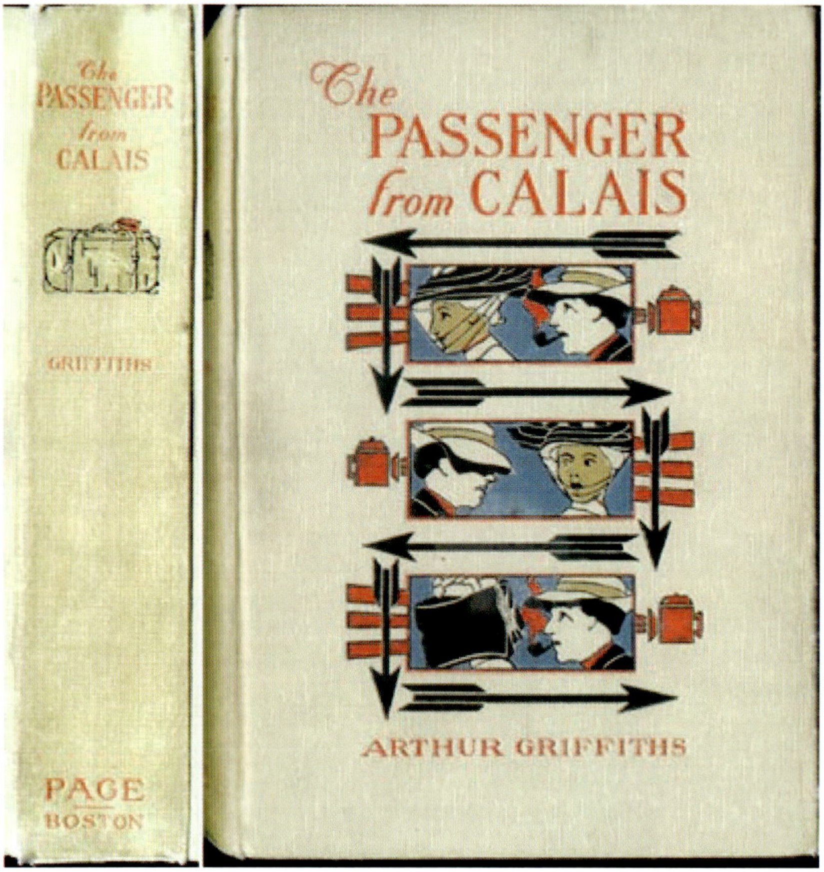

Book cover of Arthur Griffiths' *The Passenger from Calais*, 1906. (Author's collection)

His 1907 novel *The Rome Express* is set on the Rome to Paris Wagons-Lits Express. Nine passengers wake up near the end of their journey to discover that one of their number has been stabbed to death in his compartment.

> The train was travelling the last stage between Laroche and Paris, a run of a hundred miles without a stop. It had halted at Laroche for early breakfast, and many, if not all the passengers, had turned out. All had re-entered their berths to sleep or doze when the train went on, but several were on the move as it neared Paris, taking their turn at the lavatory, calling for water, towels, making the usual stir of preparation as the end of the journey was at hand.

The plot involves a wily Italian, the charming Countess di Castagneto caught in the mesh of circumstantial evidence, the chivalrous General Sir Charles Collingham and a French police force following up the wrong clues. All ends well, however, with the villain being unmasked, and the general and the countess falling in love.

Another writer of the Edwardian period who loved trains was Alfred Edward Woodley Mason (1865–1948), a Liberal Member of Parliament and author, best remembered for his 1902 novel of courage and cowardice in wartime *The Four Feathers*. His 1907 novel *Running*

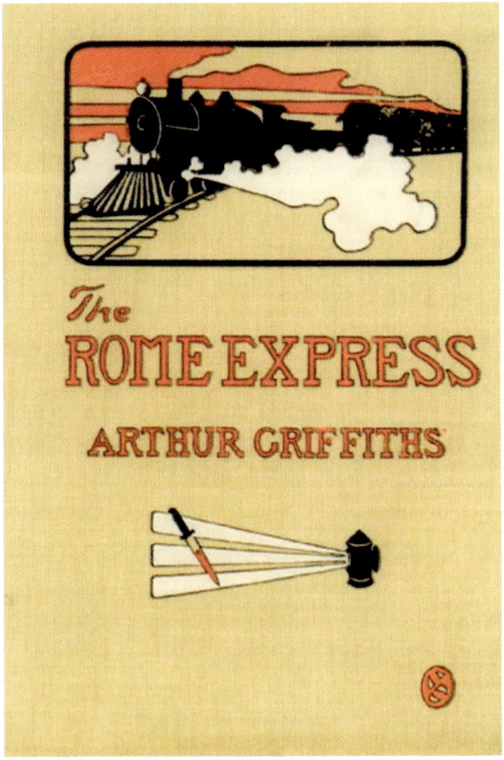

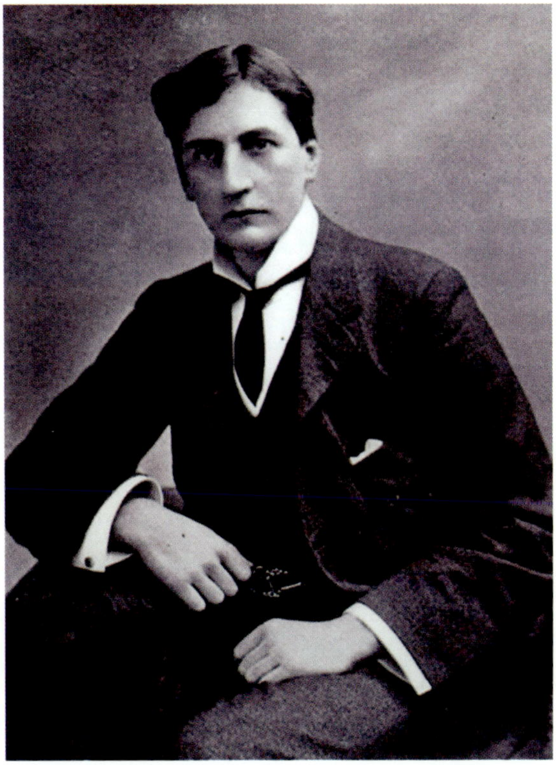

Above left: Book cover of Arthur Griffiths' *The Rome Express*, 1907. (Author's collection)

Above right: Alfred Mason (1865–1948), *c*. 1906. (Wikipedia Commons)

Water includes references to travel in a Wagons-Lits Express, and gives an evocative description of the departure of a Continental night train:

> The Geneva express jerked itself out of the Gare de Lyon. For a few minutes the lights of outer Paris twinkled past its windows and then with a sprint it reached the open night. The jolts and lurches merged into one continuous hum. ... A sleeping compartment in a Continental express was the most permanent home which Mrs Thesiger had possessed for a good many more years than she would have cared to acknowledge.

Mason's 1920 novel *The Summons*, a story of adventure and romance set before and during the First World War, recounts the adventures of Martin Hillyard, a secret service agent, and his army officer friend Harry Luttrell, and draws on the author's own experience. Chapter 15 is entitled 'In A Sleeping Car', and begins:

> The night express from Paris to Narbonne and the Spanish frontier was due to leave the Quai d'Orsay station at ten. But three quarters of an hour before that time the platform was already crowded, and many of the seats occupied. Hillyard walked

> down the steps a little before half past nine with the latest of the evening papers in his hand.... 'Will you give me your ticket, monsieur?' the porter continued. Hillyard roused himself. 'I beg your pardon. I have a compartment in the sleeping car, numbers 11 and 12.' The controller, in his brown uniform with the brass buttons and his peaked cap, stood at the steps of the car with the attendant.

Mason here gives an accurate description of the uniform worn by Wagons-Lits attendants and conjures up very effectively the rituals of departure. The action takes place in July 1916, at the height of the Battle of the Somme. Hillyard's alertness enables him to intercept secret correspondence intended for Berlin and hidden in the water tank of the lavatory by the Wagons-Lits attendant, who is in fact a German courier. The attendant is arrested and Hillyard takes the letters on with him.

Before examining the clutch of the murder/mystery novels and films associated with the Orient Express, another prestigious Continental route must be considered, that from Paris to the French Riviera. In 1883 the Compagnie Internationale des Wagons-Lits began its second luxury train after the Orient Express, travelling down to the Mediterranean coast at Nice and on to Rome. By 1890 two overnight trains were running, one via the Mont-Cenis railway to Rome, the Rome Express, and the other, the Mediterranée Express via the Rhone Valley to the Côte d'Azur.

After the First World War the train to the south of France was relaunched as the Calais-Mediterranée Express, known as the Blue Train because it was composed entirely of first-class new steel carriages (S-type), built in England and Munich, along with a dining car, all painted dark blue with a gold trim. From 1929 it ran every day, with a connecting service from London to Paris, the Flèche d'Or, or Golden Arrow. You would leave Victoria station at 11 a.m., travelling in luxurious Pullman carriages to Dover hauled by a 'King Arthur' or 'Lord Nelson' 4-6-0 engine, crossing the Channel on the SS *Canterbury* and picking up the Flèche d'Or at Calais.

The train was drawn up ready on the quayside, three or four blue and gold Pullmans, a sleeping car or two, some first-class ordinary carriages and a restaurant car. As the aperitifs

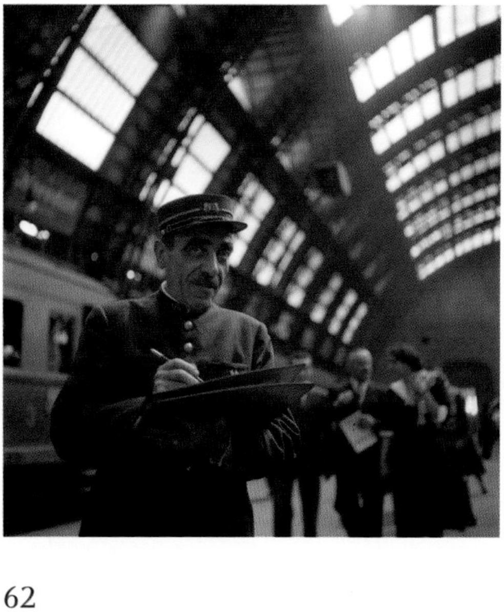

Left: Wagons-Lits Conductor Alfredo Piccinini in traditional chocolate-brown uniform welcoming passengers on board the Simplon Orient Express, 1950. He had worked for Wagons-Lits for over twenty-five years. By Jack Birns. (Shutterstock/*Life* Jack Birns)

Opposite: British Railways poster showing the international connections from Britain, including the routes to the South of France and across Europe. (Board of Trustees of the Science Museum)

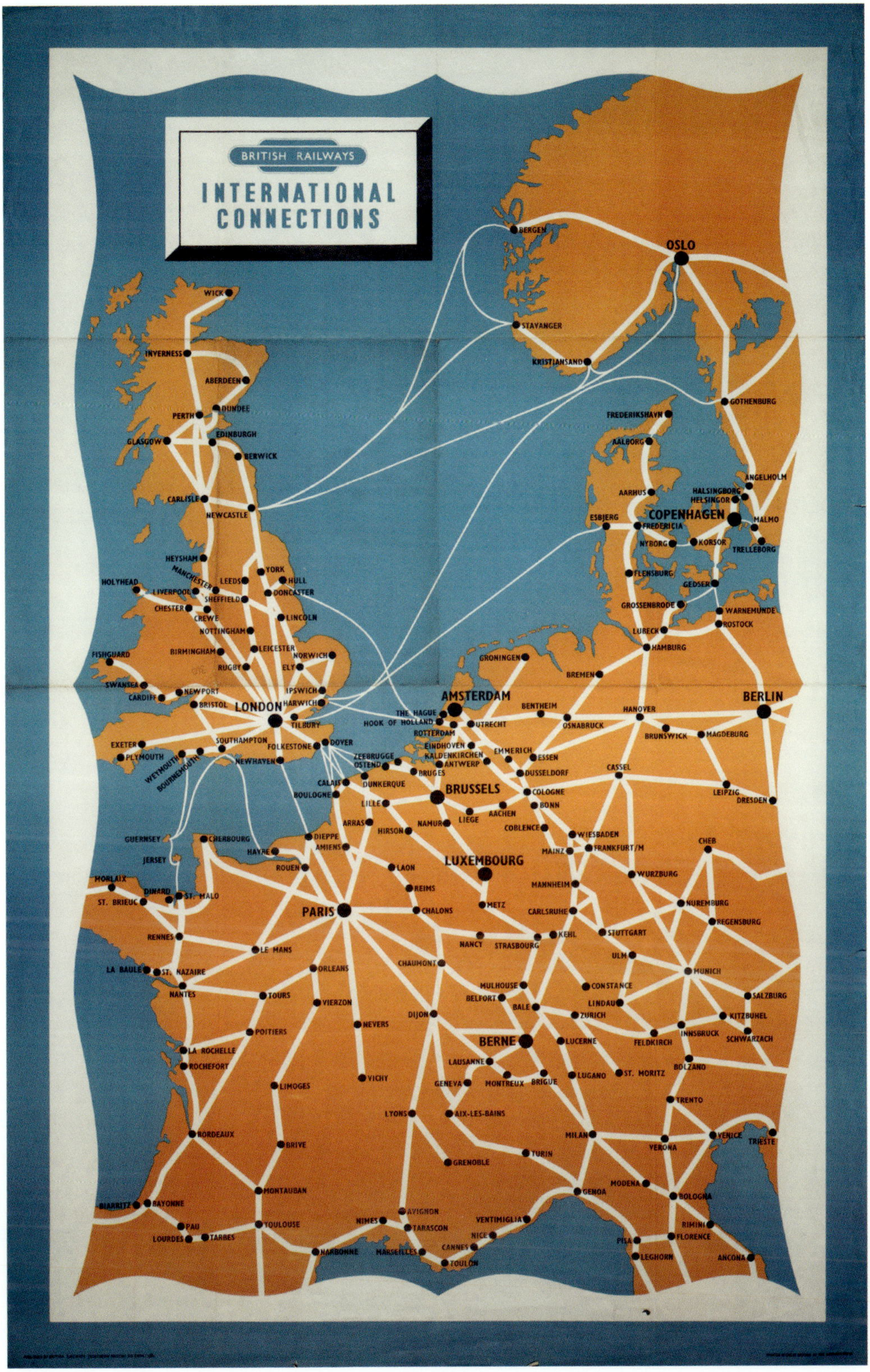
BRITISH RAILWAYS
INTERNATIONAL CONNECTIONS
WICK
INVERNESS
ABERDEEN
DUNDEE
PERTH
EDINBURGH
GLASGOW
BERWICK
CARLISLE
NEWCASTLE
HEYSHAM
MANCHESTER
LEEDS
YORK
HULL
DONCASTER
HOLYHEAD
LIVERPOOL
SHEFFIELD
CHESTER
CREWE
LINCOLN
NOTTINGHAM
BIRMINGHAM
LEICESTER
NORWICH
FISHGUARD
RUGBY
ELY
SWANSEA
CARDIFF
NEWPORT
BRISTOL
IPSWICH
HARWICH
LONDON
TILBURY
EXETER
PLYMOUTH
WEYMOUTH
BOURNEMOUTH
SOUTHAMPTON
FOLKESTONE
DOVER
NEWHAVEN
GUERNSEY
JERSEY
CHERBOURG
BERGEN
STAVANGER
KRISTIANSAND
OSLO
GOTHENBURG
FREDERIKSHAVN
AALBORG
AARHUS
HALSINGBORG
HELSINGOR
ANGELHOLM
COPENHAGEN
ESBJERG
FREDERICIA
NYBORG
KORSOR
MALMO
TRELLEBORG
FLENSBURG
GEDSER
GROSSENBRODE
WARNEMUNDE
ROSTOCK
LUBECK
HAMBURG
GRONINGEN
BREMEN
AMSTERDAM
BENTHEIM
BERLIN
THE HAGUE
HOOK OF HOLLAND
ROTTERDAM
UTRECHT
OSNABRUCK
HANOVER
BRUNSWICK
MAGDEBURG
EINDHOVEN
KALDENKIRCHEN
EMMERICH
ESSEN
ZEEBRUGGE
OSTEND
ANTWERP
BRUGES
DUSSELDORF
CASSEL
CALAIS
DUNKERQUE
BOULOGNE
BRUSSELS
COLOGNE
LEIPZIG
DRESDEN
LILLE
BONN
AACHEN
ARRAS
LIEGE
NAMUR
HIRSON
COBLENCE
WIESBADEN
DIEPPE
AMIENS
MAINZ
FRANKFURT/M
CHEB
HAVRE
ROUEN
LAON
LUXEMBOURG
WURZBURG
MORLAIX
DINARD
ST. MALO
ST. BRIEUC
REIMS
MANNHEIM
PARIS
CHALONS
METZ
NUREMBURG
CARLSRUHE
REGENSBURG
RENNES
NANCY
STRASBOURG
KEHL
STUTTGART
LE MANS
ULM
LA BAULE
ST. NAZAIRE
ORLEANS
CHAUMONT
MUNICH
NANTES
TOURS
MULHOUSE
CONSTANCE
VIERZON
BELFORT
LINDAU
SALZBURG
BALE
DIJON
ZURICH
KITZBUHEL
NEVERS
POITIERS
INNSBRUCK
BERNE
LUCERNE
FELDKIRCH
SCHWARZACH
LA ROCHELLE
ROCHEFORT
LAUSANNE
BOLZANO
VICHY
GENEVA
MONTREUX
BRIGUE
LUGANO
ST. MORITZ
LIMOGES
TRENTO
LYONS
AIX-LES-BAINS
BORDEAUX
MILAN
VERONA
VENICE
TRIESTE
BRIVE
TURIN
GRENOBLE
MODENA
GENOA
MONTAUBAN
BOLOGNA
BIARRITZ
BAYONNE
AVIGNON
VENTIMIGLIA
NIMES
TARASCON
PAU
TOULOUSE
RIMINI
LOURDES
TARBES
NICE
FLORENCE
CANNES
PISA
NARBONNE
MARSEILLES
TOULON
LEGHORN
ANCONA

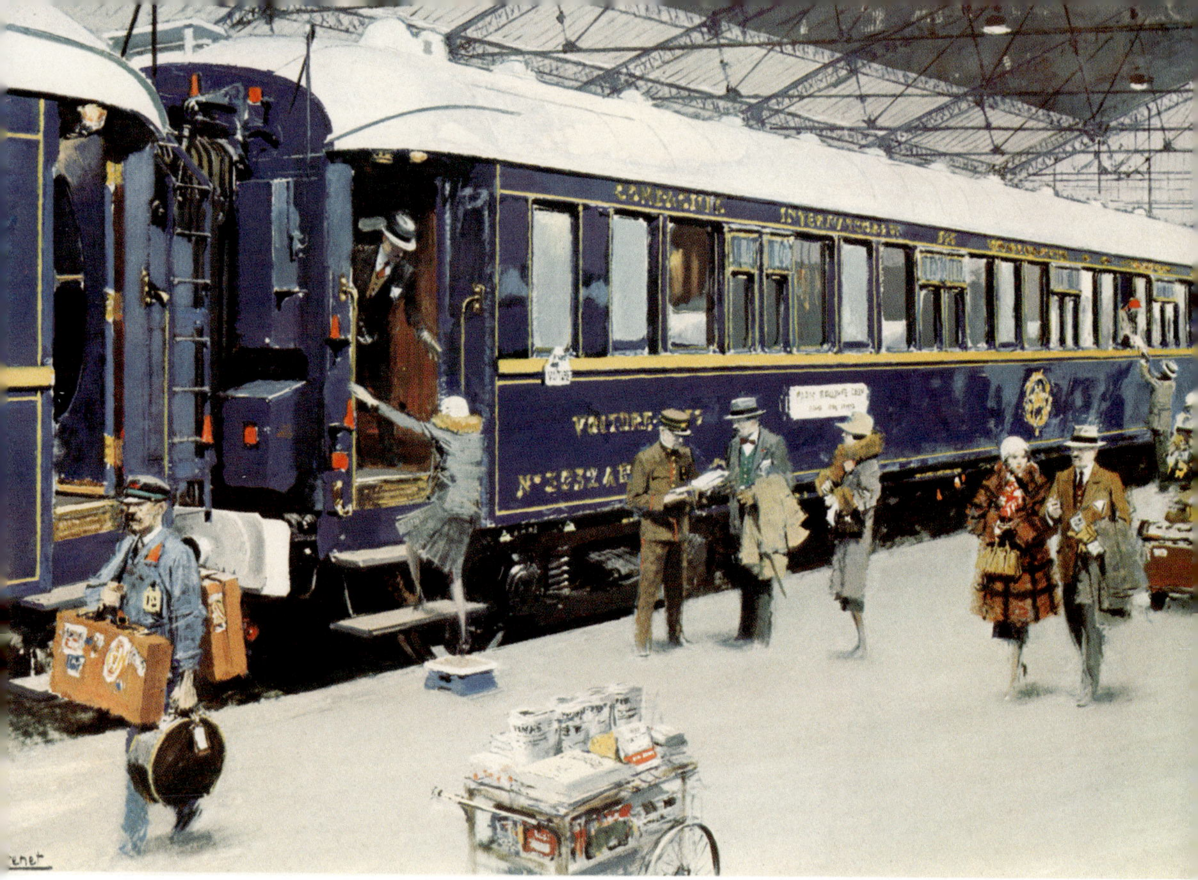

A painting in gouache by Albert Brenet of Le Train Bleu preparing for departure, 1922. It conjures up the glamour of this premier service. (Wagons-Lits Diffusion)

were being served before a late luncheon, a Nord Pacific steam locomotive would haul the train on its journey to Paris, arriving at the Gare du Nord at around 5.25 p.m.

If you were intending to connect with the Blue Train, the Wagons-Lits would be shunted off and taken to the Gare de Lyon by the Petite Ceinture, a railway line which had opened in 1854 and ran around what was then the city wall, connecting the main termini. On arrival your carriage would be attached to the ten or eleven carriages of the Blue Train before departing for the sunshine of the French Riviera. (This connection is significant when we come to examine Agatha Christie's novel *The Mystery of the Blue Train*.)

Following the popularity of this through service from England to France, in 1936 the Night Ferry was launched over the same route and using specially adapted Wagons-Lits, built in France to a smaller size than those used in Europe so that they could clear the British loading gauge. They trundled onto specially designed train ferries where passengers slept on in their cabins during the Channel crossing. The service was so popular that it was restored after the Second World War, pulled by Southern Region electric locomotives. The French attendants negotiated the formalities of passport control and the purchase of duty-free goods, so that on arrival at the Gare du Nord passengers could leave the train without any further checks, ready for their appointments in the French capital.

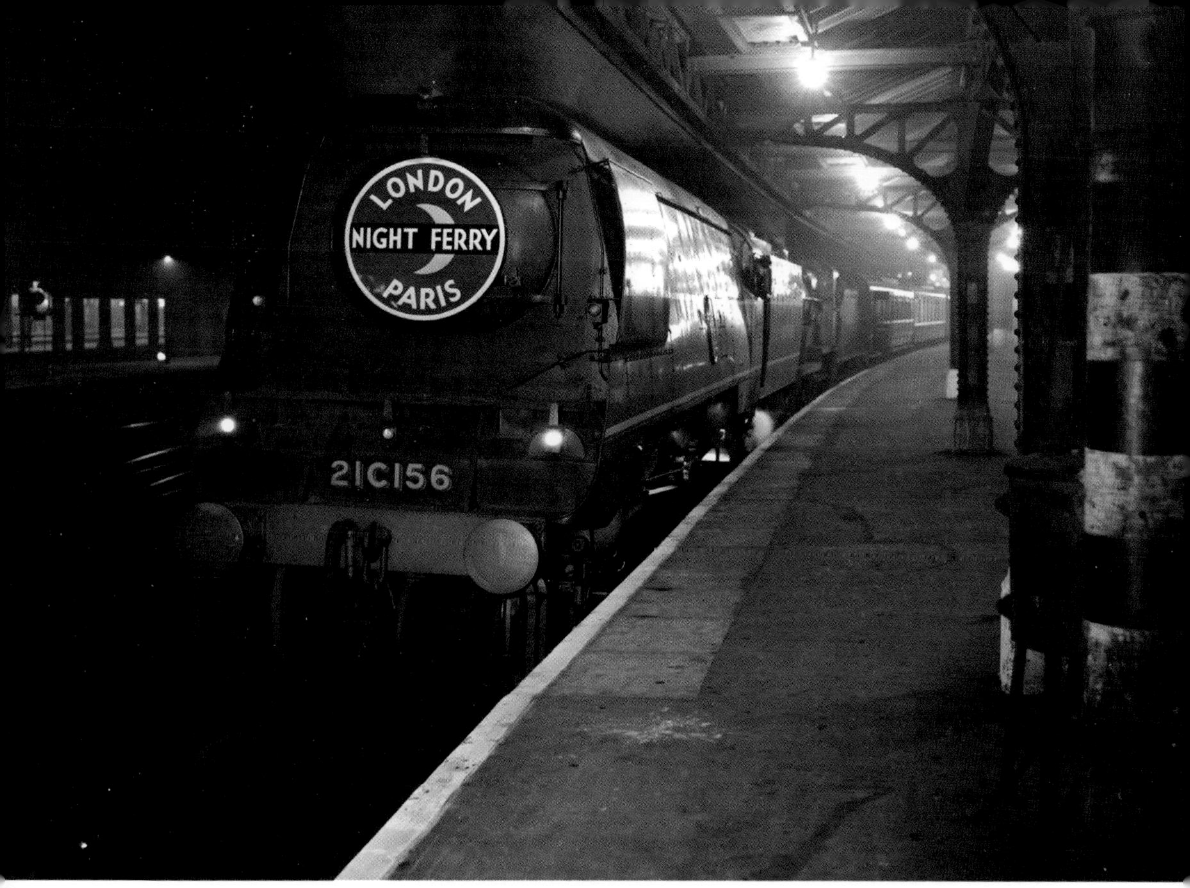

The Night Ferry at Victoria, pulled by Battle of Britain Class 4-6-2 21C 156 *Croydon*, December 1947. (Board of Trustees of the Science Museum)

In March 1928 Agatha Christie's novel *The Mystery of the Blue Train* was published by William Collins. The plot is based on an earlier short story of hers, *The Plymouth Express* (1923), and concerns the murder of an American heiress, Ruth Kettering, who is escaping her unhappy marriage to meet her lover. A famous ruby, 'The Heart of Fire', given to Ruth by her father, is found to be missing. Hercule Poirot, Christie's famous detective, is also travelling on the train, and is soon busy investigating the case, which involves mistaken identity and the puzzling fact that the killer commits the crime while the Wagons-Lit is travelling non-stop around the Petite Ceinture and then gets off the train in a way that is not explained, a serious error in the plot. Christie was sometimes careless about such details, but she conveys very effectively the luxurious atmosphere of the Blue Train, carrying the beau monde to the French Riviera during the winter months. As one of the characters says: 'Well, of course, the best train is what they call *The Blue Train*. You avoid the tiresome customs business at Calais.' Interestingly, the French novelist Arthur Bernède published *Le Mystère du Train Bleu* only a few months later, featuring a completely different plot, but probably hoping to cash in on Poirot's popularity. Christie's novel was successfully adapted for British television in 2006, starring David Suchet as Poirot.

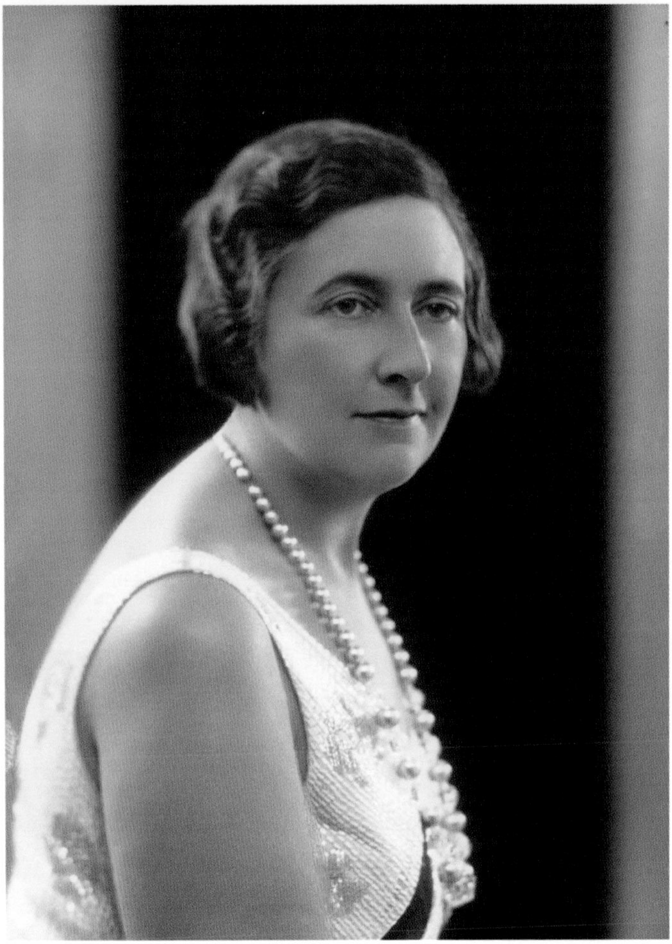

Agatha Christie (1890–1976), by Bassano Ltd, 1932. (National Portrait Gallery)

Another detective novel featuring the Blue Train is Georges Simenon's *My Friend Maigret,* published in 1949, in which Maigret is travelling from Paris to the South of France to investigate a murder. Arriving at the Gare de Lyon at around 8 p.m., he ponders whether to save money by booking a couchette, but at the last minute splashes out and buys two Wagons-Lits places instead. 'It's *The Blue Train,* Maigret mumbled, as if to excuse himself.'

Now we turn to the most famous Continental train of all, the Orient Express, on which Agatha Christie first travelled in 1928, the first of many such trips. However, before she published her novel *Murder on the Orient Express* in 1934, there had been two other mystery novels featuring the train.

The first was *La Madone des Sleepings – The Madonna of the Sleeping Cars* – by Maurice Dekobra, published in 1927, as celebrated in its own day as the James Bond books would later be, and translated into twenty-seven languages. The Madonna of the title, who became an icon for many women of the time, was a Scottish aristocrat, Winifred Grace Christabel Diana Wynham of Glensley Castle in Scotland, the daughter of the Duke of Inverness. She dabbled in psychiatry, danced naked at the Garrick Theatre in London and claimed to

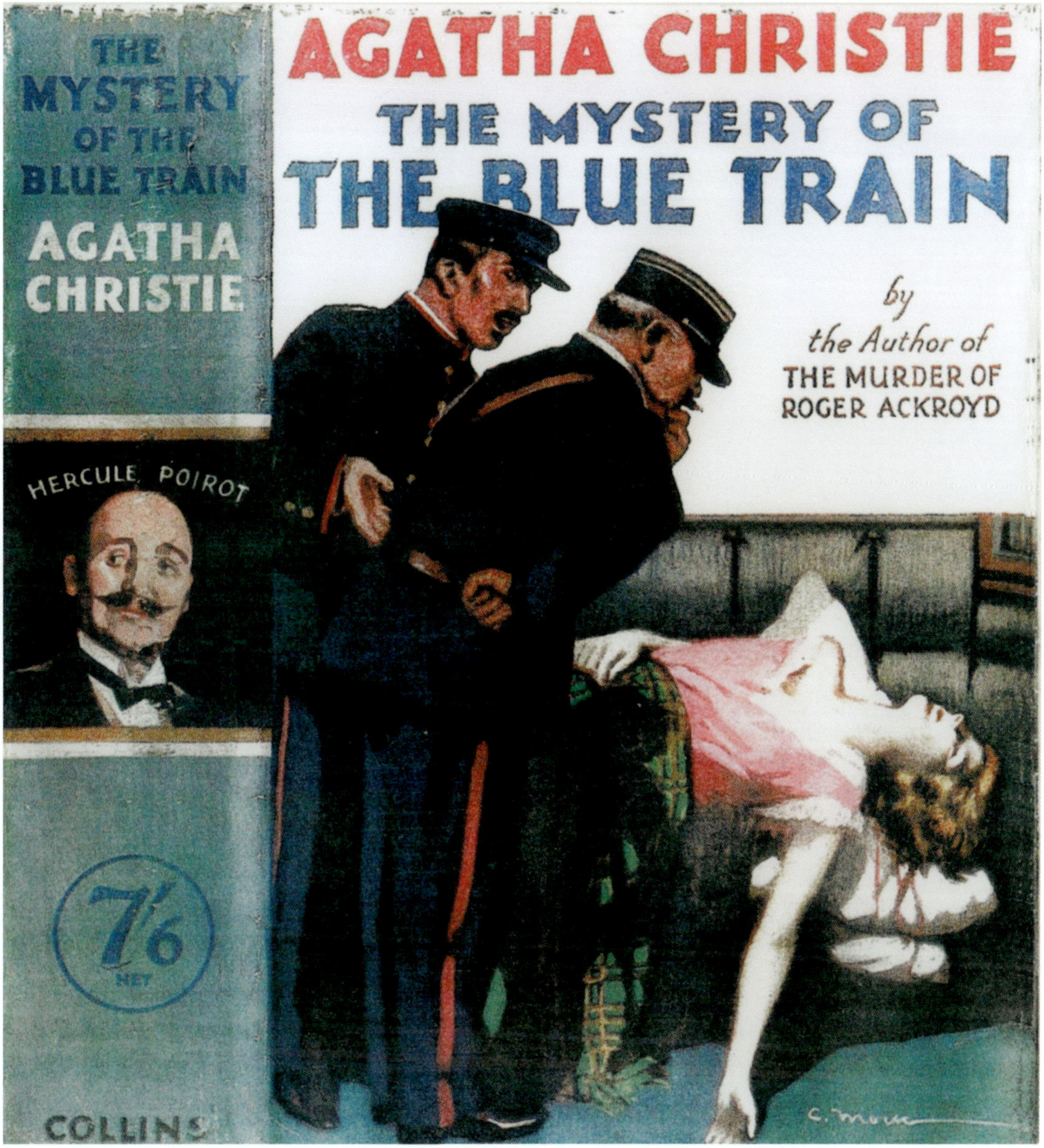

Book cover of Agatha Christie's *The Mystery of the Blue Train*, 1928. (Author's collection)

have been a Captain of Police. The plot concerns her plan to rescue rights from an oil field under the control of Communist revolutionaries, and the elimination of the evil Madame Mouravieff. Interestingly, only at the end of the story does the Orient Express feature. Lady Diana prepares to set off to the East, arriving at the Gare de l'Est to board the train. Her faithful secretary, Gèrard, Prince Seliman, describes the scene:

> I was waiting for her on the platform. It was half past one. The early arrivals were wandering through the corridors of Wagons-Lits placarded Vienna, Belgrade,

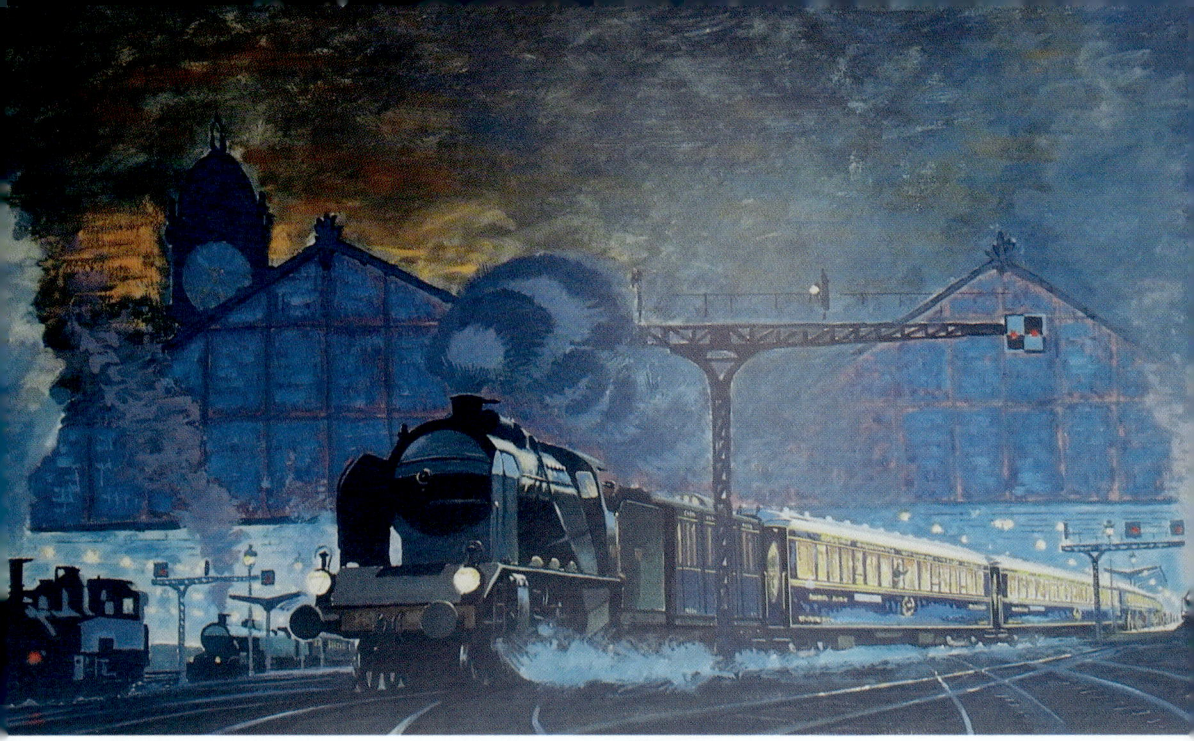

A contemporary painting of the Orient Express leaving Paris in its heyday.

Bucharest, Constantinople. Suddenly I saw a little truck laden with two valises and a toilet case of mauve crocodile, which I recognised. I spied Lady Diana following the porter. She was a symphony in pearl grey, from her tiny hat, stabbed through with a diamond ornament, to the tips of her little shoes of alligator skin.

Lady Diana, togged out for a long voyage, tripped lightly along the sunny platform. ...

The hour of departure was imminent. Whistles were screeching and excited arms were tossing valises through the open windows. The car was swallowing baggage and vomiting the friends of travellers.

Lady Diana had said to him, 'I'm sure that you've heard all about the hundreds of miles which I have covered on Continental railroads. A French humorist had the audacity to call me "The Madonna of the Sleeping Cars".... As a matter of fact, I have been in every European watering place: there is not a Customs officer who doesn't know the most sacred details of my lingerie. They say that to go away is to die a little, but it's my idea that to die would be to go too far, and that to travel is simply to change one's ideas.'

'My eyes,' wrote Gèrard, Prince Seliman, 'followed the rails along which the train had disappeared, the *train de luxe* bearing the "Madonna of the Sleeping Cars" towards a new destiny.'

The Orient Express train is a much more central feature in Graham Greene's *Stamboul Train*, published in 1932. Greene includes details in the novel that are based on his own

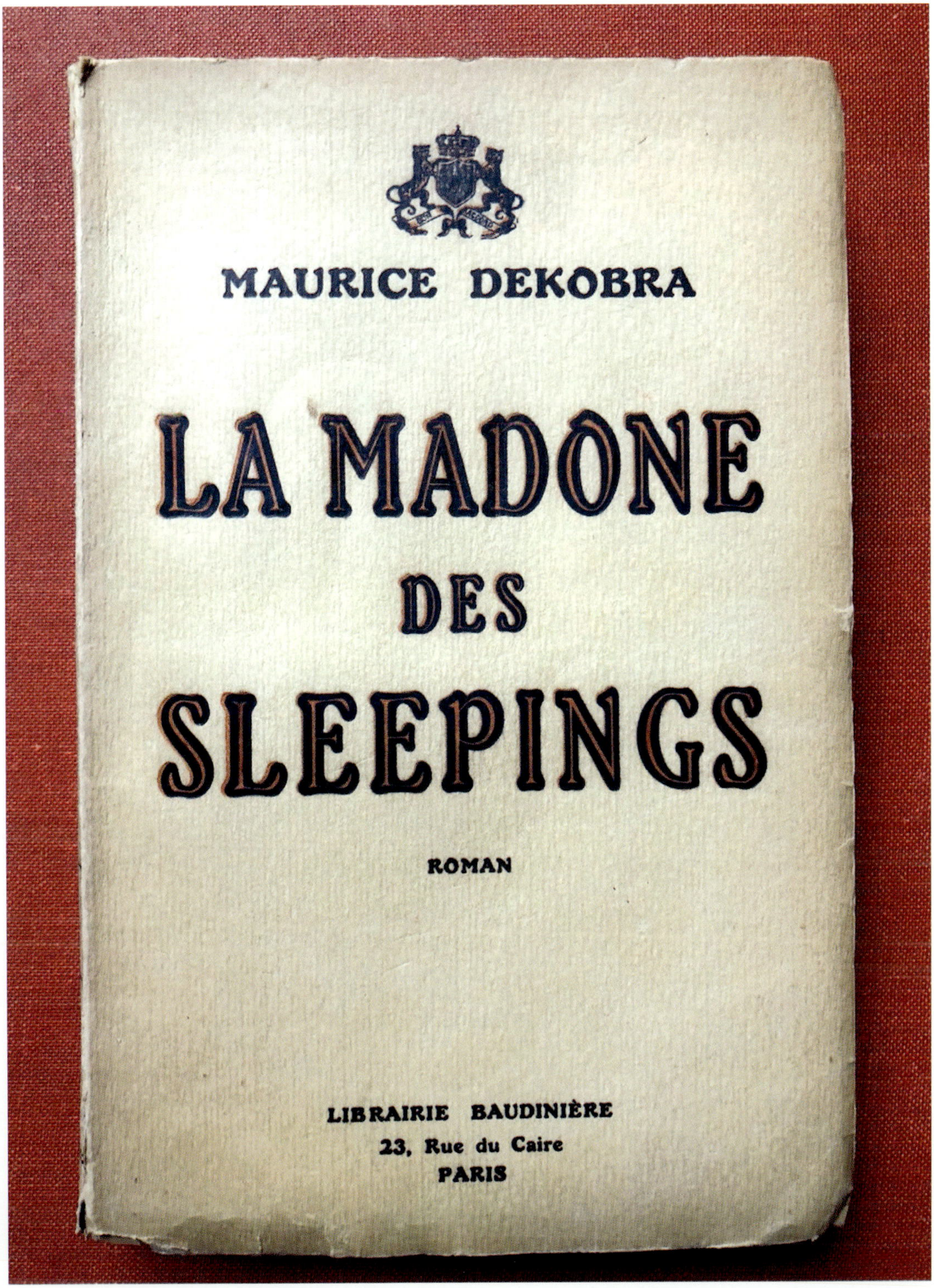

Book cover of Maurice Dekobra's *La Madone des Sleepings*: first edition, 1925. (Wikipedia Commons)

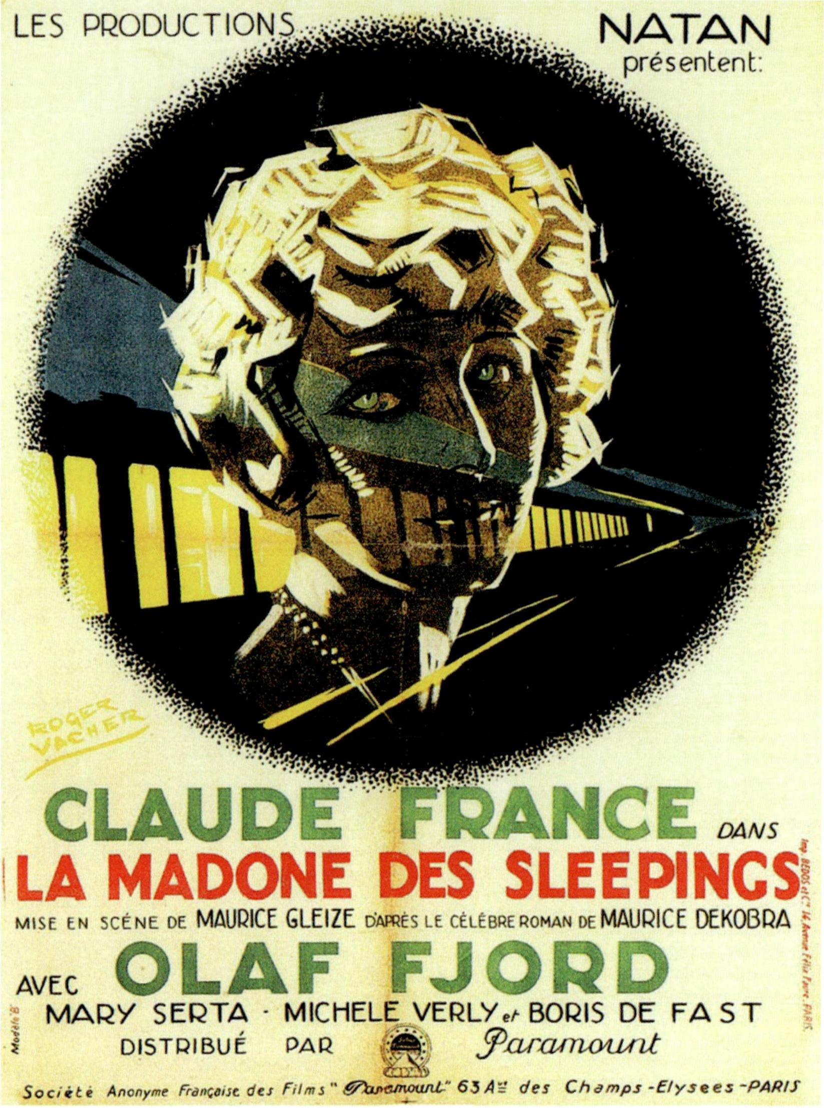

Poster for the 1928 silent film *La Madone des Sleepings,* starring Claude France and Olaf Fjord. (Wikipedia Commons)

experiences, and in his memoir *Ways of Escape* mentions that on a train journey to Cologne he took copious notes of what he saw, which he wove into the book.The story takes place on a three-day journey from Ostend to Constantinople via Subotica and most of the action takes place on the train, with evocative descriptions of train noises and smells, the seedy stations and frontier posts in the middle of the night lit only by oil lamps.

The main figure is Coral Musker from Nottingham who joins Carleton Myatt, a Jewish businessman, Mr Peters and his wife, the notorious Dr Czinner, the author Quin Savory and later Mabel Warren and Janet Pardoe, and the escaped criminal Josef Grünlich.

Throughout the journey Greene conjures up the feeling of the landscape, the interactions of the passengers and an underlying sense of disquiet.

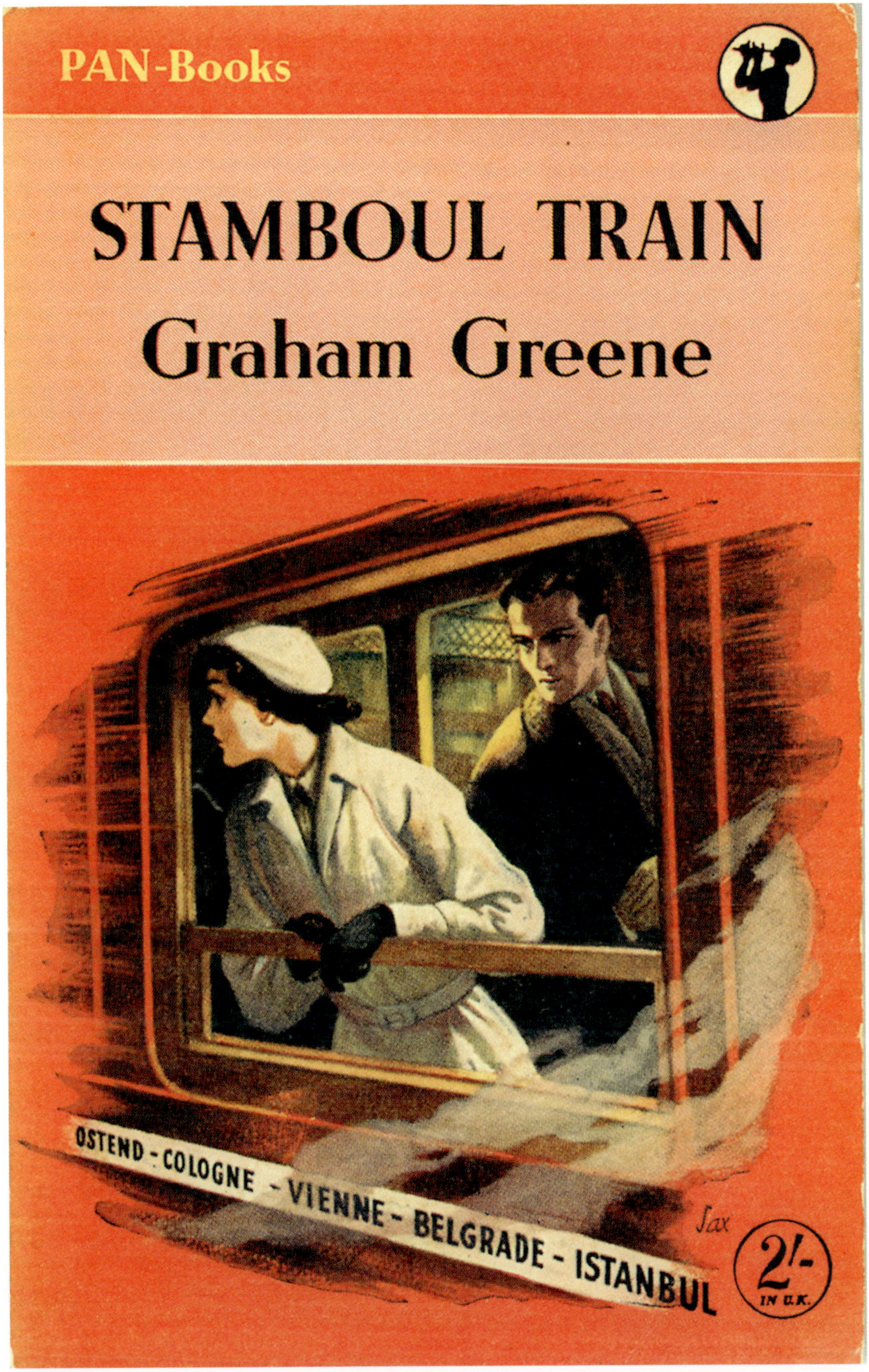

Book cover of Graham Greene's *Stamboul Train*, 1932. The cover of the first UK paperback edition was by R. M. Sax, who designed book jackets for Pan Books between 1951 and 1957. The image shows Coral Musker looking out of the carriage window, with Carleton Myatt in the background. (Author's collection)

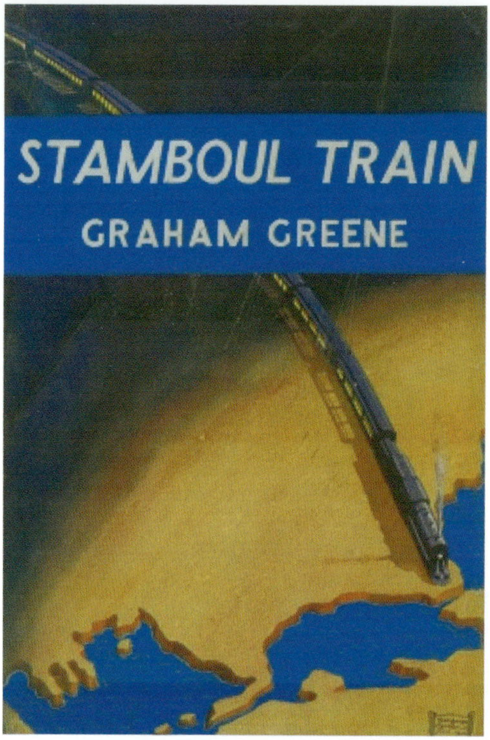

The cover of the first edition of Graham Greene's *Stamboul Train*, 1932, designed by Philip Youngman Carter, and showing the Orient Express crossing Europe to the Bosporus.

As the train moves off ...

> The driver turned his regulator full open, and the footplate shook with the weight of the coaches. Presently the engine settled smoothly to its work, the driver brought the cut-off back, and the last of the sun came out as the train passed through Bruges, the regulator closed, coasting with steam ... The sparks of the express became visible, like hordes of scarlet beetles tempted into the air by night; they fell and smouldered by the track, touched leaves and twigs and turned to soot.

Greene combines vividly observed technical detail with a compelling sense of urgency as the train moves inexorably forward:

> The great blast furnaces of Liège rose along the line like ancient castles burning in a border raid. The train lurched and the points clanged. Steel girders rose on either side, and very far below an empty street ran diagonally into the dark, and a lamp shone on the café door. The rails opened out, and unattached engines converged on the express, hooting and belching steam. The signals flashed green across the sleepers, and the arch of the station roof rose above the carriage. Newsboys shouted, and a line of stiff sedate men in black broadcloth and women in black veils waited along the platform; without interest, like a crowd of decorous strangers at a funeral, they watched the line of first class coaches pass them, Ostend—Cologne—Vienne—Belgrade—Istanbul—the slip-coach for Athens.

Later, as they travel further east, the snow begins to fall, and as the lights of Vienna flash past, Greene conjures up the inconsequential conversations in the restaurant car, as well as the sudden silences:

> All down the restaurant cars fell the sudden concerted silence which is said to mean that an angel passes overhead. But through the human silence the tumblers tingled on the table, the wheels thudded along the iron track, the windows shook and sparks flickered like match-heads through the darkness ...

There has been a murder in Vienna, and the murderer is now on the train. At the frontier station of Subotica the drama reaches its climax with the arrest of Czinner, Grünlich and Coral, and the subsequent denouement. Finally the train arrives at the dingy Sirkeci station in Constantinople, where there is a resolution of sorts, but in typical Greene style not a conventional happy ending.

Stamboul Train was an instant success, prompting Greene to hope that it would be made into a film, although at first he wasn't very hopeful. As he comments in his memoir *Ways of Escape*, 'others had beaten him to it'; Marlene Dietrich had appeared in *Shanghai Express*, the English had made *Rome Express* and even the Russians had produced their railway film *Turksib*.

However, two years after *Stamboul Train* had been published in the United States as *Orient Express*, in 1934 a film of the novel was released using the American title. This posed a problem for Agatha Christie, whose novel about the Orient Express was published in the same year. So, the British edition was given the title *Murder on the Orient Express* while it was published as *Murder in the Calais Coach* in the United States. Christie's novel is however quite different to Graham Greene's.

Christie loved train travel, ever since she had decided on a whim in 1928 to take the Orient Express to visit the ancient city of Ur in modern Iraq to recover from the trauma of her divorce from Archibald Christie, her first husband. She describes in her archaeological memoir *Come Tell Me How You Live* (1946) the excitement of her departure from Victoria station in London:

> Dear Victoria – gateway to the world beyond England – how I love your continental platform. And how I love trains ... Snuffling up the sulphurous smell ecstatically ... A big snorting, hurrying, companionable train, with its big puffing engine, sending up clouds of steam, and seeming to say impatiently 'I've got to be off!'

Later, in Chapter One of her memoir she confides:

> Many, many years ago, when going to the Riviera or to Paris, I used to be fascinated by the sight of the Orient Express at Calais and longing to be travelling by it. Now it has become an old familiar friend, but the thrill has never quite died down. I am going by it! I am *in* it! I am actually in the blue coach, with the simple legend outside: CALAIS-ISTANBUL. It is, undoubtedly, my favourite train. I like its tempo, which, starting *Allegro con furore*, swaying and rattling and hurling one from side to side in its mad haste to leave Calais and the occident, gradually slows down in a *rallentando* as it proceeds eastwards till it becomes definitely *legato*.

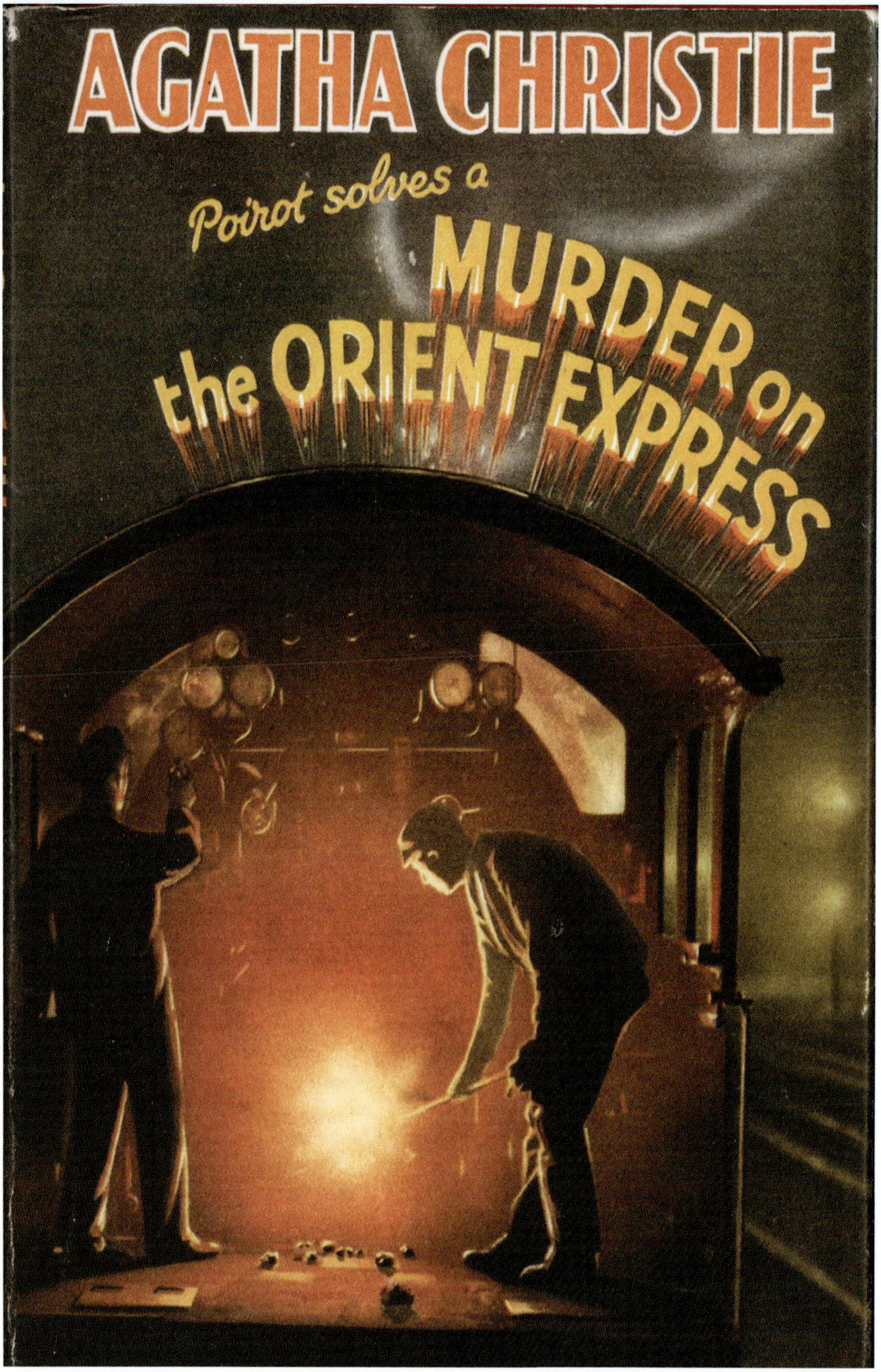

Book cover of Agatha Christie's *Murder on the Orient Express*, 1934. (Author's collection)

The pace gets slower and slower, the stops are longer, the station clocks display conflicting times. The names of the stations are written in exciting and improbable-looking letters. The engines are fat and comfortable-looking, and belch forth a particularly black and evil smoke.

Over the years Christie travelled frequently on the Orient Express to the archaeological sites in the Middle East where her husband Professor Max Mallowan worked, and the story of her novel begins in the Middle East with Hercule Poirot boarding the train, bound for Calais and London. In Greene's novel the train travels in the opposite direction. Christie begins her tale: 'It was five o'clock on a winter's morning in Syria. Alongside the platform at Aleppo stood the train grandly designated in railway guides as the *Taurus Express*. It consisted of a kitchen car, a sleeping car, and two local coaches.' The Wagons-Lits company already had a restaurant car and two sleeping cars running

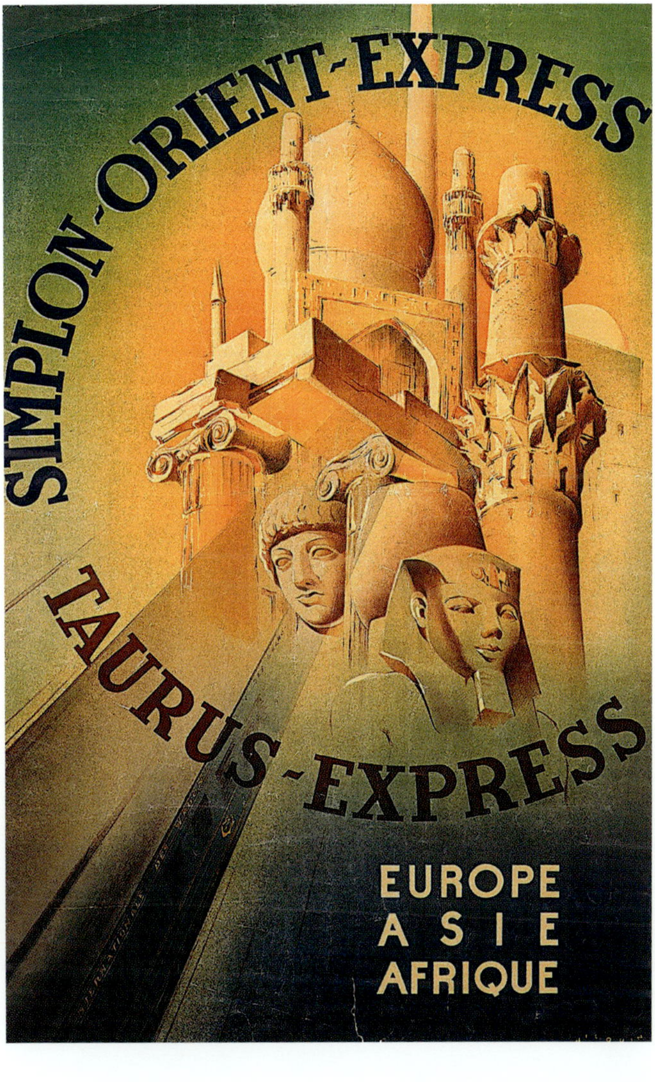

Poster for the Simplon Taurus Express, subtitled 'Europe Asie Afrique'. (CIWL archive (c Wagons-Lits Diffusion Phototeque))

between Cairo and Port Said, but because of the publicity attached to the discovery of the tomb of Tutankhamun by Howard Carter in November 1922 the company was soon planning to link the Orient Express with the Cairo Express, establishing a railway line from Eskisehir to Aleppo, which then divided, one line continuing east to Baghdad and the other heading south to Cairo. It opened in 1930 and was known as the Taurus Express. A contemporary poster advertised London to Baghdad in eight days, with 'safety, rapidity and economy guaranteed'.

The Taurus Express ran into Haydarpasa station on the Asian side of the Bosphorus, which sat right on the seafront, from where passengers crossed to the European side by special ferry and made their way to Sirkeci station for the onward journey. Comparing the two novels it is also clear that both writers chose slightly different Orient Express routes. While Greene's novel begins at Ostend with the train travelling via Cologne to Vienna, Christie makes Poirot travel on the Simplon Orient Express which travels via Belgrade and Trieste to Paris via the Simplon Tunnel. Greene deals with darker themes than Christie, including anti-Semitism, a political uprising in Yugoslavia and sexual exploitation. Most interesting from the perspective of this book is the treatment of the train itself. Greene makes it a more normal setting for travel, downplaying the glamour and peopling it with frankly quite seedy characters, while for Christie the Orient Express is a luxurious sealed world, full of exotic and stylish characters including rich Americans and an elderly Russian princess, a place of escapism in which the murder/mystery can unfold. In the 1974 film version of the novel, directed by Sidney Lumet and starring among others Lauren Bacall, Ingrid Bergman, Sean Connery and Vanessa Redgrave, the

Haydarpasa station, Constantinople, 1958. The station was built in 1908 on the shores of the Bosphorus, from where the Taurus Express ran south to Baghdad, Aleppo and Beirut. (Board of Trustees of the Science Museum)

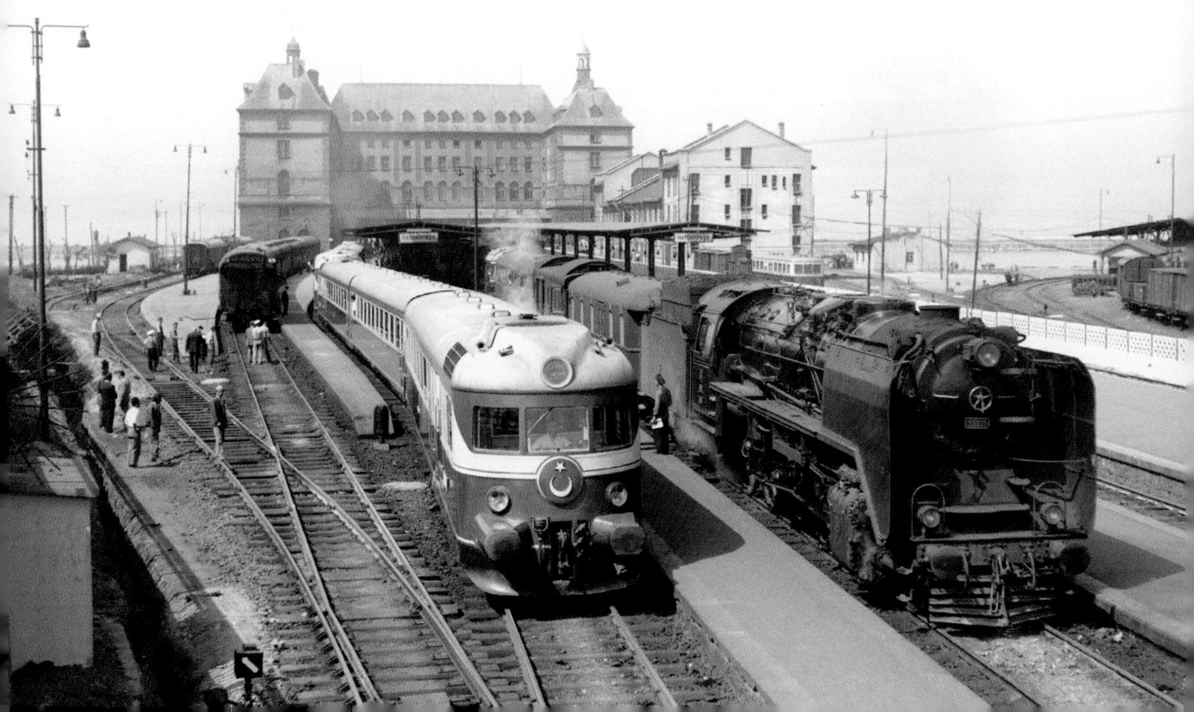

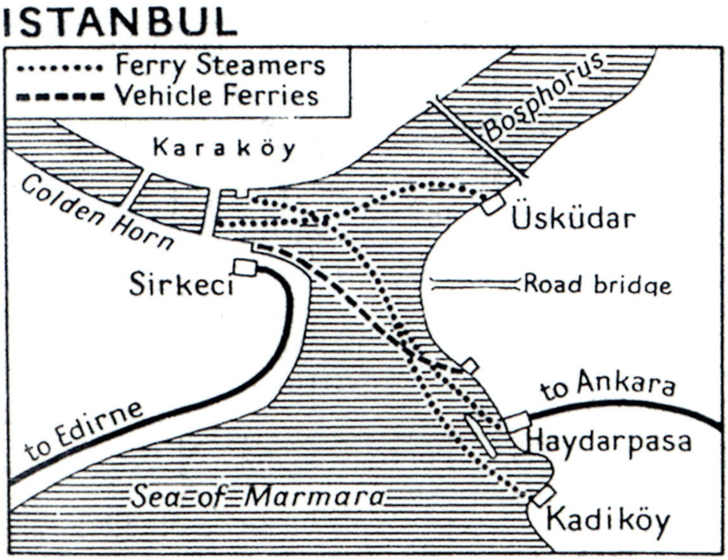

Right: Plan of Istanbul, showing the position of the two railway stations on each side of the Bosphorus. From Thomas Cook's International Rail Timetable. (Author's collection)

Below: Wagons-Lits carriages as part of the Venice Simplon Orient Express Luxury Train.

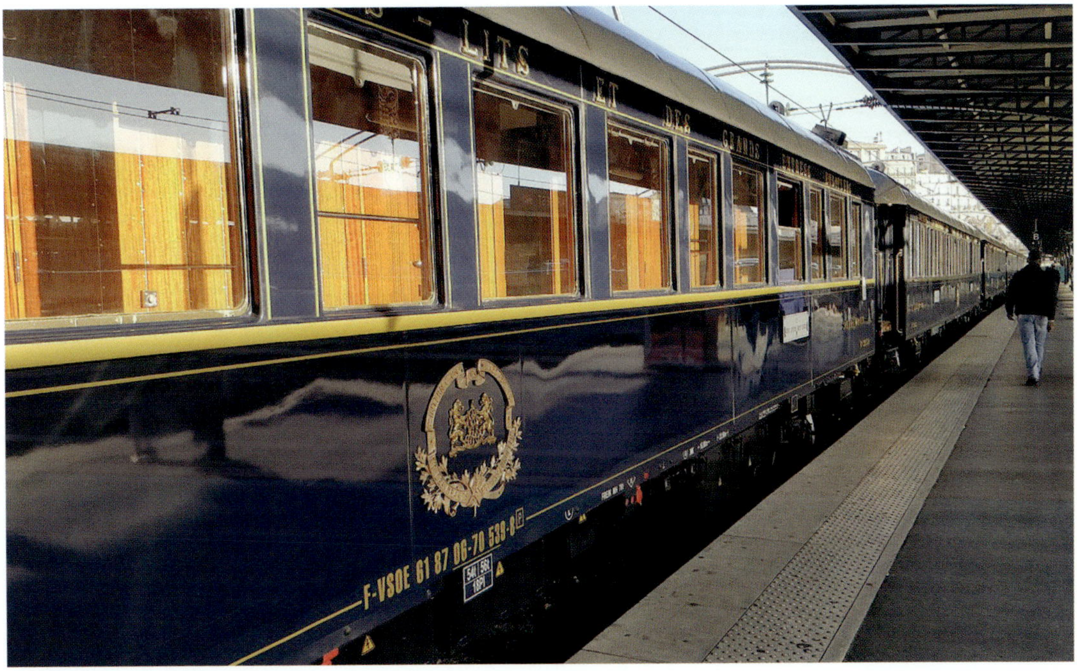

train is almost fetishised, beautifully presented with the music swelling to a climax as it starts its journey and begins to move.

When Poirot boards the train at Sirkeci station he finds that the Wagons-Lits are all booked, but eventually room is found for him in berth No. 7. He dines sumptuously at a favoured table in the restaurant car, surrounded by the other passengers, including Princess Dragomiroff, Samual Ratchet, alias Cassetti, Mrs Hubbard, Mary Debenham,

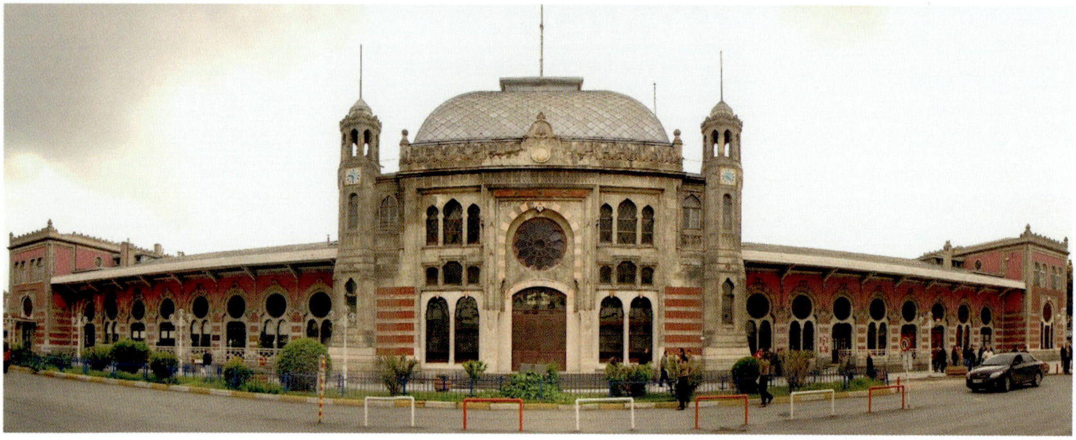

Sirkeci station, Istanbul, the end of the line for the Orient Express. (CIWL archive (c Wagons-Lits Diffusion Phototeque))

Colonel Arbuthnot and the others, twelve in all. As Monsieur Bouc, a director of the Wagons-Lits company, reflects:

> All around us are people, of all classes, of all nationalities, of all ages. For three days these people, these strangers to one another, are brought together. They eat and sleep under one roof, they cannot get away from each other. At the end of three days they part, they go their several ways, never, perhaps, to see each other again.
>
> 'And yet'; said Poirot, 'suppose an accident—'

The action takes place between the Athens–Paris coach and the restaurant car when the train gets stuck in a snowdrift after Belgrade, between Vincovci and Brod, where a murder is discovered, and Poirot is called on to investigate. After questioning all the passengers, Poirot proposes two possible solutions before retiring from the case.

Christie's novel was inspired partly by the kidnapping of Charles Lindbergh's twenty-month-old son, who was held for ransom in 1932, and partly by an incident in 1929 when the Orient Express was trapped in a blizzard at Çerkezköy in Turkey and marooned for ten days. A Mrs Beth Vinding, who was trapped on the train with her four-year-old son, wrote an account of their ordeal. After nine days stuck at Alpullu station, with only one proper meal each day, a snowplough arrived and the train began moving forward, only for the snowplough itself to become derailed.

> ... we became really very worried. It looked as though we were going to have to sit it out until the snow melted with no friendly sugar mill to sell us food. Fortunately our fears were groundless as the snow plough was put back on the rails and slowly, very slowly, we crawled safely into Stambul. For the first time in a fortnight we washed, had a good meal and slept in a hotel room which, after the cramped train compartment, seemed truly gigantic. It was certainly a journey I shall never forget.

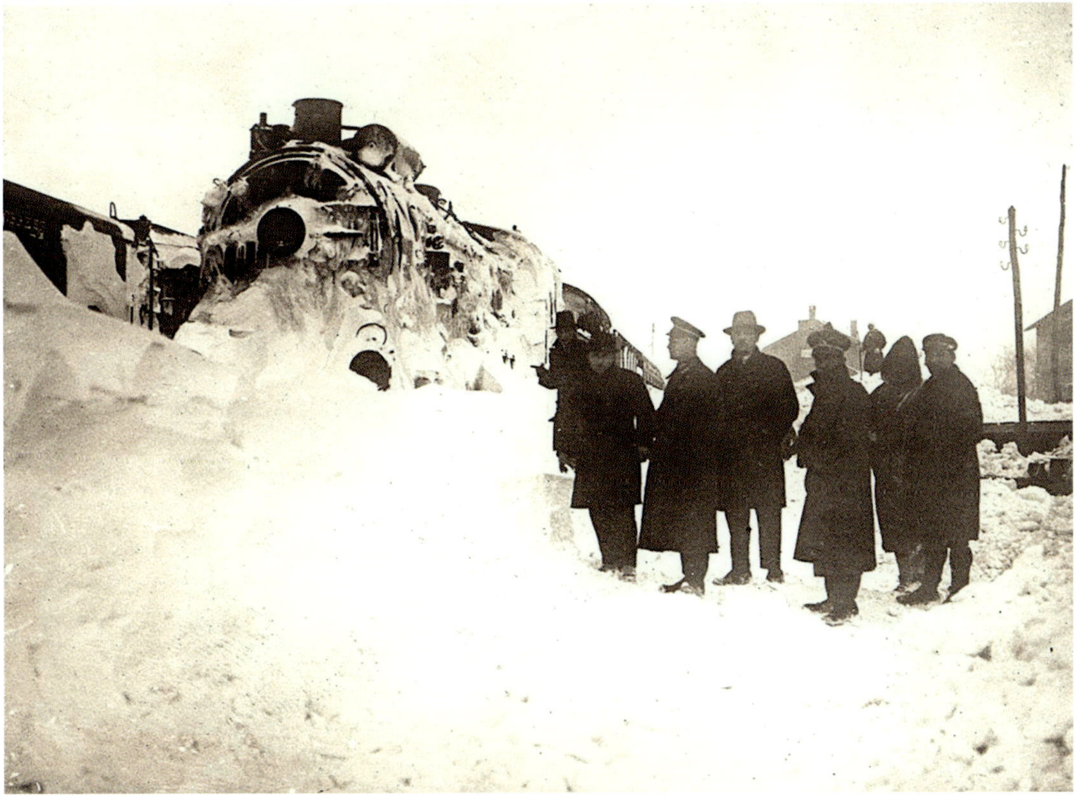

The Orient Express stuck in a snowdrift at Çerkezköy in Turkey, February 1929. (CIWL archive (c Wagons-Lits Diffusion Phototeque))

The sleeping car in which she was travelling, No. 3309, has survived and is still in use today on the luxury Belmond Venice Simplon Orient Express.

Christie's attention to detail is evident throughout the novel. She checked cabin layouts, the position of door handles and switches, and even provided a diagram of the carriage layout in the book. The story still ranks as one of the most popular Agatha Christie novels, and there have been many film and TV adaptations.

Other writers capitalised on this successful formula, including an American, A. den Doolaard, who wrote *Express to the East* in 1936, which concerns Milja, a courier for a secret society involved in the civil war between the Turks and the Serbs. Cecil Roberts wrote *Victoria, Four-Thirty* in 1937, set on the Arlberg-Orient Express, the first European express to be reinstated after the Second World War, but whose origin goes back to the Treaty of Versailles in 1919, when it followed the Simplon-Orient route to Vienna, later extended to Bucharest and on to Athens.

William McGivern, an American novelist who began work as a police reporter, and who published mystery thrillers, wrote a short story in 1952 about the Orient Express, *The Sound of Murder*. The action takes place at the Yugoslav/Trieste border, at Sesana, where Adam James, travelling to Belgrade, hears an argument in the next compartment between a Serbian couple. While Adam is in the restaurant car the conductor comes to tell the

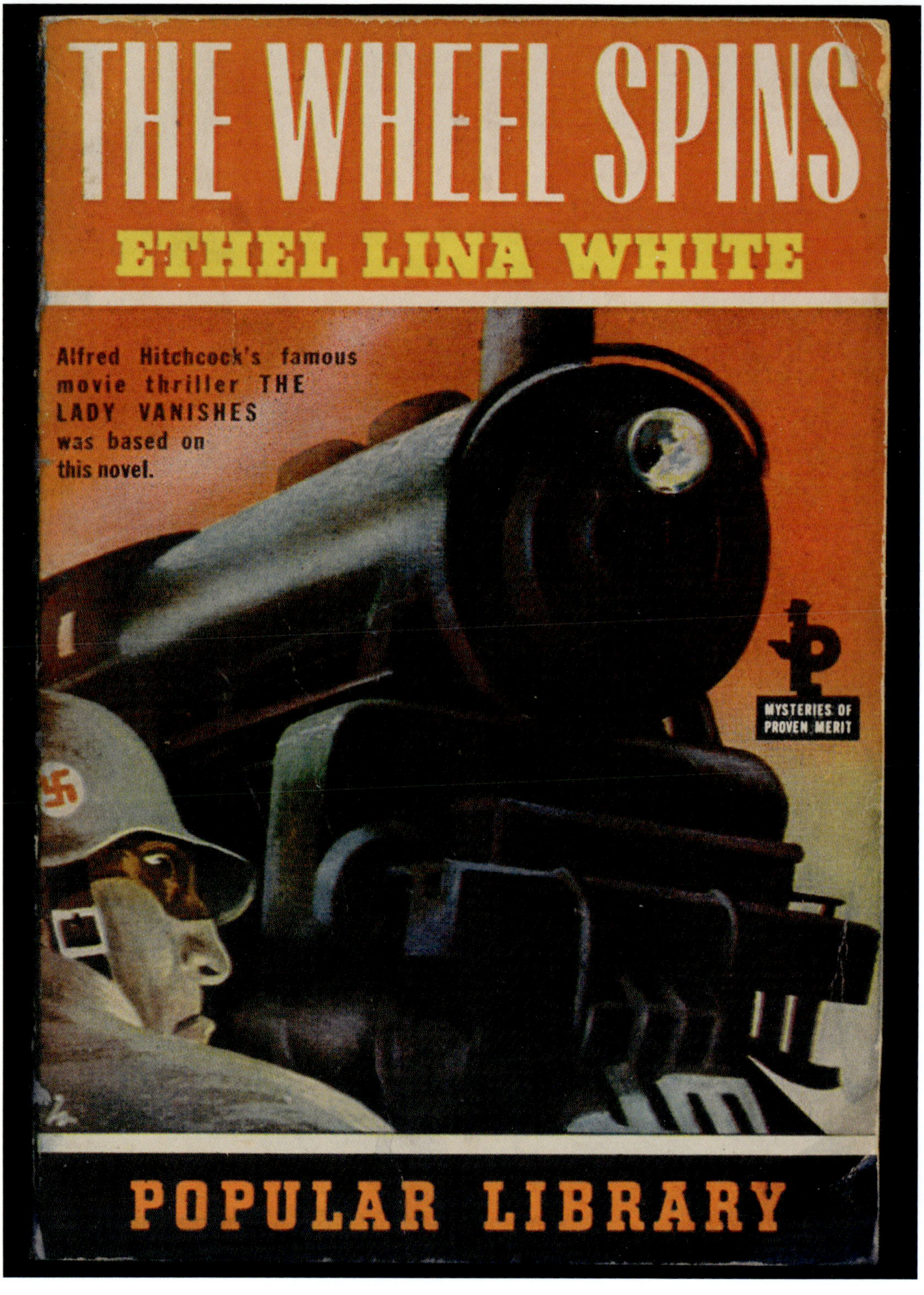

Book cover of Ethel Lina White's *The Wheel Spins,* paperback edition, 1944. Artwork by Hoffmann.

Serbian, Duvec, that his wife has been stabbed and a soldier is under arrest for the murder. Adam takes charge, convinced that the soldier is innocent, and unmasks the killer.

One of the best-known crime writers in Britain and America in the 1930s and 1940s was Ethel Lina White (1876–1944), who gave up her work for the Ministry of Pensions in 1919 to become a full-time writer. She is remembered for her novel *The Wheel Spins*, published in 1936, on which Alfred Hitchcock's 1938 film *The Lady Vanishes* is based.

White's story concerns a young lady, Iris Carr, who travels from 'a remote corner of Europe' to Trieste, on the overnight train, to pick up the Orient Express to Calais. After an incident at the station when she briefly loses consciousness, she boards the train and finds herself in a compartment with Miss Winifred Froy, an English governess going home to England on holiday, and an imperious lady dressed in black, the Baroness, to whom Miss Froy seems to be under some kind of obligation. Returning from lunch in the restaurant car Iris falls asleep, and when she wakes up Miss Froy is no longer there. All her fellow passengers deny ever having seen her, but there is a mysterious heavily bandaged passenger in the next compartment, attended by a sinister-looking doctor and his assistant. Iris is befriended by a fellow passenger, Max Hare, who wants to help her but is persuaded by the doctor that Iris is suffering mentally and needs to be given a sleeping

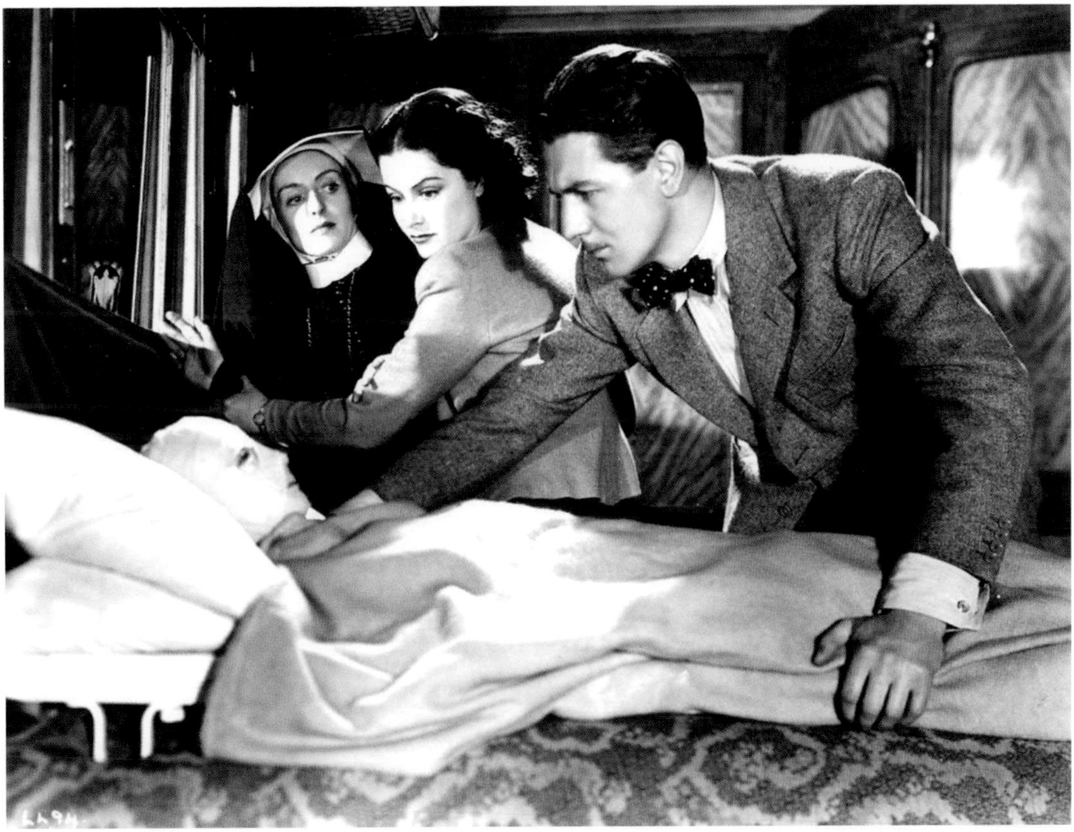

Film still from *The Lady Vanishes*, directed by Alfred Hitchcock, 1938, starring Margaret Lockwood, Michael Redgrave, Basil Radford and Catherine Lacey. (Wikipedia Commons)

draught to help calm her down. However, as it takes effect she is given the strength to enter the next compartment and rip off the bandages from the 'patient', who indeed turns out to be Miss Froy, who had been targeted because she was a witness to the Baroness's plans. The doctor and his assistant are arrested, but Max believes that the Baroness will use her influence to have the matter hushed up.

The book has a somewhat stilted style, but it does conjure up the tension of a train travelling inexorably to its destination and carrying the fate of those on board with it. Before Iris boards the train, she is awakened in her hotel by the express thundering through the valley and curving round the edge of the lake:

> In imagination, she saw it shooting through Europe, as though it were an explosive shuttle ripping through the scorched fabric of the map. It caught up cities and threaded them on a gleaming whistling string. Illuminated names flashed before her eyes and were gone – Bucharest, Zagreb, Trieste, Milan, Basle, Calais.

In Hitchcock's film Miss Froy becomes a secret service agent bringing a stolen code out of the Balkans, and although sleeping cars are not mentioned in the film script, they do briefly feature. The film plot differs considerably from White's novel, where the wheel keeps spinning, the train doesn't stop and there are no scenes of shooting and violence. However, the film was an immediate hit at the box office, and is regarded as one of the wittiest and most accomplished of Hitchcock's British films.

Our tour of murder/mystery novels and films set on the Orient Express comes to a satisfying conclusion with the second film in the James Bond series, *From Russia with Love,* which premiered in 1963, starring Sean Connery. It was based on Ian Fleming's novel, the fifth of his Bond novels, published in 1957.

The idea for the book came to Fleming from two main sources. In June 1955 he had travelled to Istanbul to cover an Interpol conference as a journalist for the *Sunday Times,* where he met Oxford-educated ship owner Nazim Kalkavan, who became the inspiration for Darko Kerim, and when he returned home he travelled by the Orient Express, although he found it a rather depressing experience.

Fleming also knew about the true story of Eugene Karp, an American naval attaché and friend of Robert Vogeler, an American businessman who was later jailed for espionage in Hungary. Karp, who was an intelligence agent based in Budapest, took the Orient Express in February 1950 from Budapest to Paris, carrying papers about blown American spy networks behind the Iron Curtain. However, there were Soviet assassins already on the train, the conductor was drugged and Karp was pushed to his death. His body was found in a railway tunnel near Saltzburg. Fleming enjoyed trains and used them in several of his novels. The background to the novel was the intensifying Cold War between Russia and the West, and the story revolves around Bond's mission to defeat Soviet secret agents and seize hold of a Spektor, a Russian decoding device.

Bond travels to Istanbul to meet a Soviet defector, Tatiana Romanova, and bring back the Spektor. While there he meets Darko Kerim, head of the British service station in Turkey, and together they board the Orient Express, on which the three Russian secret agents are travelling. Like Maurice Dekobra's *The Madonna of the Sleeping Cars,* this is another novel where the train only makes its appearance towards the end of the book.

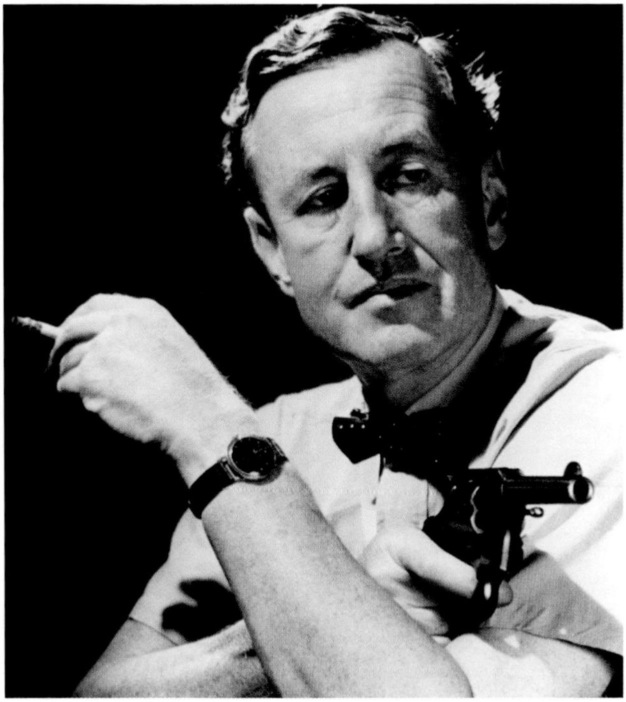

Ian Fleming (1908–64), the author of the James Bond series of spy novels.

Fleming is as good as Graham Greene at evoking the atmosphere of the Continental express trains:

> The great trains are going out all over Europe, one by one, but still, three times a week, the *Orient Express* thunders superbly over the 1,400 miles of glittering steel track between Istanbul and Paris. ... Under the arc-lights, the long-chassied German locomotive panted quietly with the laboured breath of a dragon dying of asthma. Each heavy breath seemed certain to be the last. Then came another. Wisps of steam rose from the couplings between the carriages and died quickly in the warm August air. The *Orient Express* was the only live train in the ugly, cheaply architectured burrow that is Istanbul's main station. The trains on the other lines were engineless and unattended—waiting for tomorrow. Only Track No. 3, and its platform, throbbed with the tragic poetry of departure....
>
> The heavy bronze cipher on the side of the dark blue coach said 'COMPAGNIE INTERNATIONALE DES WAGONS-LITS ET DES GRANDS EXPRESS EUROPEENS'. Above the cipher, fitted into metal slots, was a flat iron sign that announced, in black capitals on white, ORIENT EXPRESS, and underneath, in three lines:
>
> | | | |
> |---|---|---|
> | ISTANBUL | THESSALONIKI | BEOGRAD |
> | VENEZIA | MILAN | |
> | LAUSANNE | PARIS | |
>
> James Bond gazed vaguely at one of the most romantic signs in the world.

As the train pounds through the night, making its way out of Turkey, Fleming paints a vivid picture of the train's movement in the darkness:

> ... the hasty metal gallop of wheels, the hypnotic swoop of the silver telegraph wires, the occasional melancholy, reassuring moan of the steam whistle clearing their way, the drowsy metallic clatter of the couplings at each end of the corridor, the lullaby creak of the woodwork in the little room.

Fleming conjures up images of wayside stations in the Balkans, with their low platforms, seedy buildings and scruffy officials, as the train travels through the vaguely menacing countryside of Yugoslavia. As the train pulls into Thessaloniki station, the faithful Kerim is found murdered, and at Trieste the killer, Captain Donovan Grant, formerly of the Royal Corps of Signals and now Chief Executioner of SMERSH, joins the train. After drugging Romanova, he confronts Bond, telling him that he is going to be shot as the train enters the Simplon Tunnel. There is a struggle between Bond and Grant in the confined space of the sleeping compartment, in which Grant is killed, and Bond leaves the train at Dijon at 5.30 a.m.

Before their fight, Grant taunts Bond by describing how the Orient Express is a perfect vehicle for a spy thriller: 'man, the story's got everything. *Orient Express.* Beautiful Russian spy murdered in Simplon Tunnel. Filthy pictures: Secret Cipher machine. Handsome British spy with career ruined murders her and commits suicide. Sex, spies, luxury train ... Old Man, it'll run for months!' The 1963 film, produced by Albert Broccoli and Harry Saltzman, follows the story reasonably faithfully, except for the ending where Fleming's ambiguous conclusion is replaced with something more cinematically satisfying. It is a much more austere and less action-packed film than later films in the series, but with its splendid theme tune sung by Matt Munro, its brisk pace, tight plot and its gritty quality this is often considered to be the best of the Bond films.

Epilogue

'The Great Trains are Going Out All Over Europe, One by One'

Not many years after the film *From Russia with Love* came out, the Orient Express ceased to run. The age of the great express trains criss-crossing Europe was slowly coming to an end.

When I was a teenager in 1965 I travelled to Greece with my brother and two friends by train, on a shoe-string budget using a student travel organisation called Brian Hughes Travel. Brian was an enterprising Oxford undergraduate who booked railway compartments to and from Athens. We picked up the train at Ostend and travelled in couchettes to Munich, where after a six-hour stop, we transferred to the Tauern Orient Marmara Express via Zagreb, Belgrade, Skopjë and Thessaloniki down to Athens. In spite of its exotic name, the train's accommodation was now more spartan, just an ordinary day compartment which the four of us occupied, determined to fend off any later passengers trying to join us. At night we slept two on the seats and two in the luggage racks. From Salzburg we enjoyed the magnificent views of the Austrian Tyrol, with narrow mountain passes and a glimpse of a chateau perched on top of a hill. We crossed the border into Yugoslavia at 10.45 p.m. that evening, and once over the border everything became more primitive, the train ran more slowly and we passed through the grim city of Skopjë, shattered by the devastating earthquake of 1963, which killed over a thousand people and destroyed 80 per cent of the buildings. Later on, we encountered great drama when a child playing on the line was hit by the train and was put in the luggage car to be taken to hospital. We never discovered whether she survived. The countryside was flat, with the occasional village, muddy roads and carts drawn by horses or oxen. Children herded flocks of sheep along the dirt tracks, women and children stacked hay and on the railway line we encountered splendid steam locomotives, sporting a mass of complicated pipework and hissing steam and puffs of smoke.

Beyond Skopjë we climbed up between high mountains, the line clinging to the side of a spectacular gorge and then descended into a fertile plain where cypress and pine trees were growing. At Gevgelija, the Yugoslav border station, we paused for half an hour while our passports and luggage were checked, a procedure repeated at Idomeni, where loud

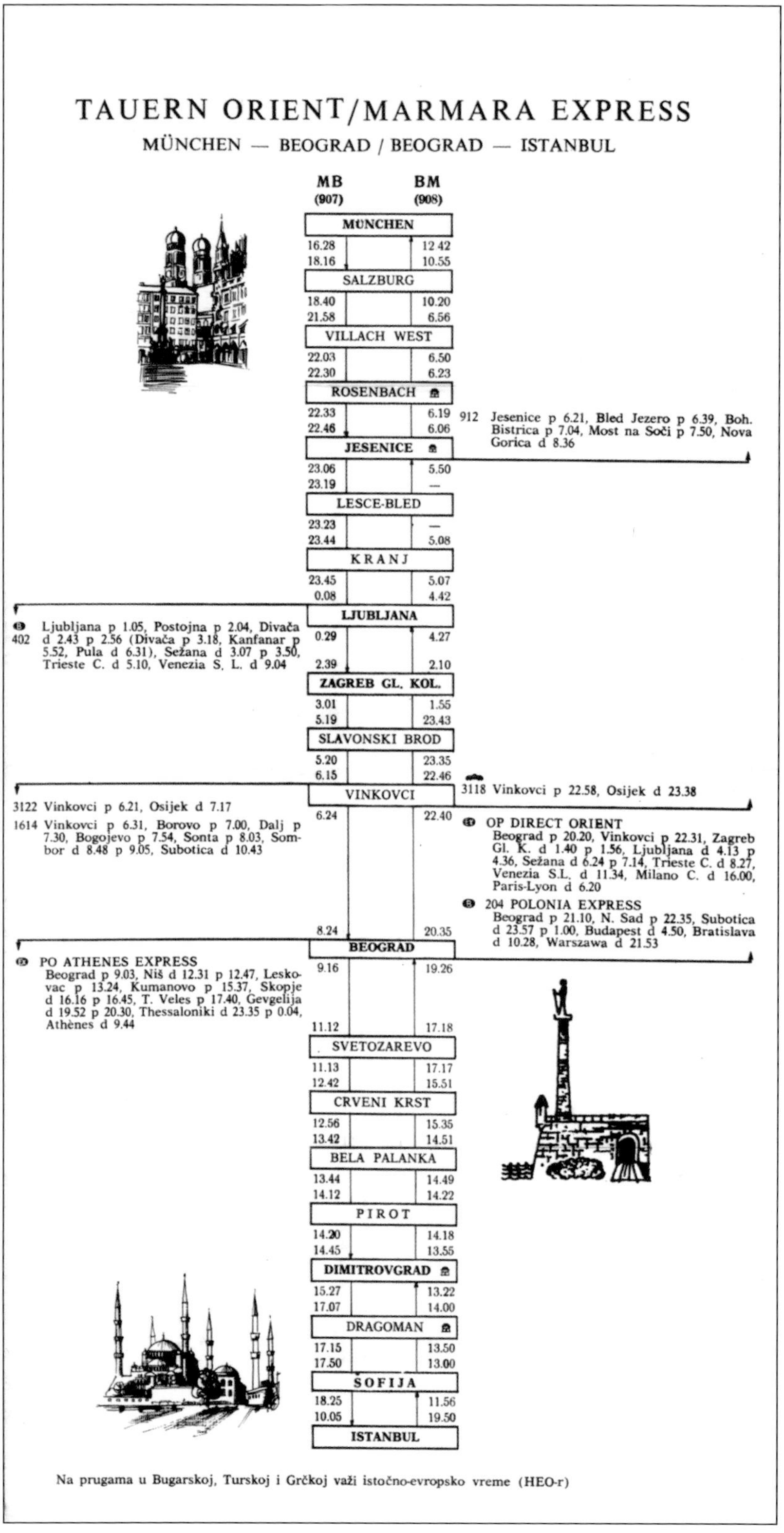

TAUERN ORIENT/MARMARA EXPRESS

MÜNCHEN — BEOGRAD / BEOGRAD — ISTANBUL

	MB (907)	BM (908)
MÜNCHEN		
	16.28	12 42
	18.16	10.55
SALZBURG		
	18.40	10.20
	21.58	6.56
VILLACH WEST		
	22.03	6.50
	22.30	6.23
ROSENBACH		
	22.33	6.19
	22.46	6.06
JESENICE		
	23.06	5.50
	23.19	—
LESCE-BLED		
	23.23	—
	23.44	5.08
KRANJ		
	23.45	5.07
	0.08	4.42
LJUBLJANA		
	0.29	4.27
	2.39	2.10
ZAGREB GL. KOL.		
	3.01	1.55
	5.19	23.43
SLAVONSKI BROD		
	5.20	23.35
	6.15	22.46
VINKOVCI		
	6.24	22.40
	8.24	20.35
BEOGRAD		
	9.16	19.26
	11.12	17.18
SVETOZAREVO		
	11.13	17.17
	12.42	15.51
CRVENI KRST		
	12.56	15.35
	13.42	14.51
BELA PALANKA		
	13.44	14.49
	14.12	14.22
PIROT		
	14.20	14.18
	14.45	13.55
DIMITROVGRAD		
	15.27	13.22
	17.07	14.00
DRAGOMAN		
	17.15	13.50
	17.50	13.00
SOFIJA		
	18.25	11.56
	10.05	19.50
ISTANBUL		

912 Jesenice p 6.21, Bled Jezero p 6.39, Boh. Bistrica p 7.04, Most na Soči p 7.50, Nova Gorica d 8.36

402 Ljubljana p 1.05, Postojna p 2.04, Divača d 2.43 p 2.56 (Divača p 3.18, Kanfanar p 5.52, Pula d 6.31), Sežana d 3.07 p 3.50, Trieste C. d 5.10, Venezia S. L. d 9.04

3118 Vinkovci p 22.58, Osijek d 23.38

3122 Vinkovci p 6.21, Osijek d 7.17

1614 Vinkovci p 6.31, Borovo p 7.00, Dalj p 7.30, Bogojevo p 7.54, Sonta p 8.03, Sombor d 8.48 p 9.05, Subotica d 10.43

OP DIRECT ORIENT
Beograd p 20.20, Vinkovci p 22.31, Zagreb Gl. K. d 1.40 p 1.56, Ljubljana d 4.13 p 4.36, Sežana d 6.24 p 7.14, Trieste C. d 8.27, Venezia S.L. d 11.34, Milano C. d 16.00, Paris-Lyon d 6.20

204 POLONIA EXPRESS
Beograd p 21.10, N. Sad p 22.35, Subotica d 23.57 p 1.00, Budapest d 4.50, Bratislava d 10.28, Warszawa d 21.53

PO ATHENES EXPRESS
Beograd p 9.03, Niš d 12.31 p 12.47, Leskovac p 13.24, Kumanovo p 15.37, Skopje d 16.16 p 16.45, T. Veles p 17.40, Gevgelija d 19.52 p 20.30, Thessaloniki d 23.35 p 0.04, Athènes d 9.44

Na prugama u Bugarskoj, Turskoj i Grčkoj važi istočno-evropsko vreme (HEO-r)

Timetable and route map of the Tauern Orient Marmara Express, 1968. (Author's collection)

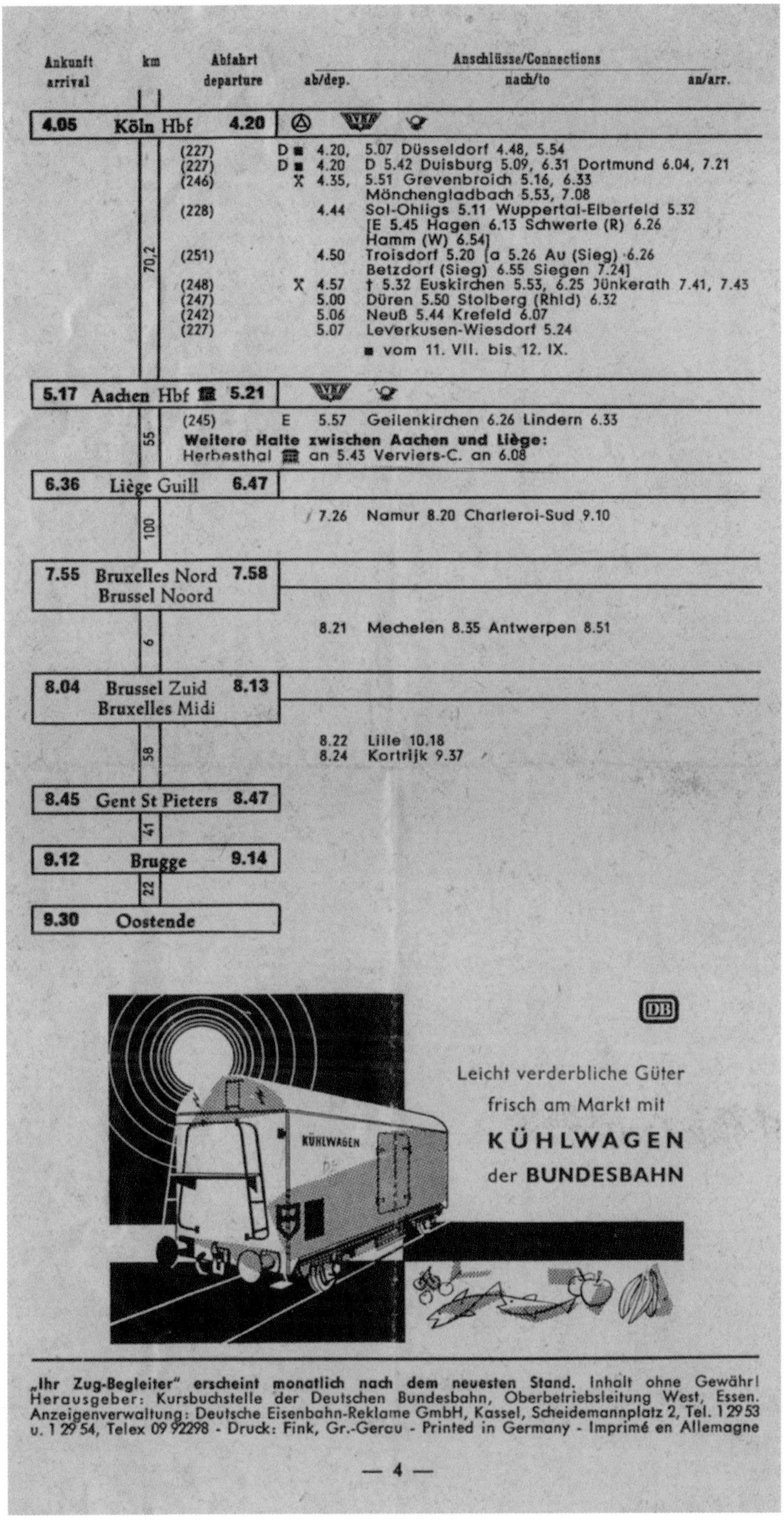

Ankunft arrival	Station	Abfahrt departure	km	Anschlüsse/Connections ab/dep.	nach/to – an/arr.
4.05	Köln Hbf	**4.20**			
				(227) D 4.20,	5.07 Düsseldorf 4.48, 5.54
				(227) D 4.20	D 5.42 Duisburg 5.09, 6.31 Dortmund 6.04, 7.21
				(246) ✗ 4.35,	5.51 Grevenbroich 5.16, 6.33 Mönchengladbach 5.53, 7.08
				(228) 4.44	Sol-Ohligs 5.11 Wuppertal-Elberfeld 5.32 [E 5.45 Hagen 6.13 Schwerte (R) 6.26 Hamm (W) 6.54]
			70,2	(251) 4.50	Troisdorf 5.20 [a 5.26 Au (Sieg) 6.26 Betzdorf (Sieg) 6.55 Siegen 7.24]
				(248) ✗ 4.57	† 5.32 Euskirchen 5.53, 6.25 Jünkerath 7.41, 7.43
				(247) 5.00	Düren 5.50 Stolberg (Rhld) 6.32
				(242) 5.06	Neuß 5.44 Krefeld 6.07
				(227) 5.07	Leverkusen-Wiesdorf 5.24
					vom 11. VII. bis 12. IX.
5.17	Aachen Hbf	**5.21**			
			55	(245) E 5.57	Geilenkirchen 6.26 Lindern 6.33
					Weitere Halte zwischen Aachen und Liège: Herbesthal an 5.43 Verviers-C. an 6.08
6.36	Liège Guill	**6.47**			
			100	7.26	Namur 8.20 Charleroi-Sud 9.10
7.55	Bruxelles Nord / Brussel Noord	**7.58**			
			6	8.21	Mechelen 8.35 Antwerpen 8.51
8.04	Brussel Zuid / Bruxelles Midi	**8.13**			
			58	8.22	Lille 10.18
				8.24	Kortrijk 9.37
8.45	Gent St Pieters	**8.47**			
			41		
9.12	Brugge	**9.14**			
			22		
9.30	Oostende				

„Ihr Zug-Begleiter" erscheint monatlich nach dem neuesten Stand. Inhalt ohne Gewähr! Herausgeber: Kursbuchstelle der Deutschen Bundesbahn, Oberbetriebsleitung West, Essen. Anzeigenverwaltung: Deutsche Eisenbahn-Reklame GmbH, Kassel, Scheidemannplatz 2, Tel. 12953 u. 12954, Telex 0992298 - Druck: Fink, Gr.-Gerau - Printed in Germany - Imprimé en Allemagne

— 4 —

Timetable for the journey from Münich to Ostend on the Tauern Express. (Author's collection)

Bouzouki music was playing to welcome us to Greece. We had depended entirely on buying food from the stations at which we stopped, and as we travelled down through northern Greece, past Thermopylae and Levadia, the temperature began to rise.

After three nights of little sleep and meagre rations we were very relieved to reach the blistering August heat of Athens as the train pulled into Larissa station, and to crash out in the modest Hotel Marion.

As far as I know there were no murderers or spies on our train, but I still have the travel timetables we used, following roughly the route Graham Greene mapped out in *Stamboul Train*, a reminder that the original Orient Express routes remained in use, even though the trains lacked the luxury and style of a previous age.

When Andrew Martin's book *Night Trains* was published in 2017, the great Continental night trains had long gone, and even the regular overnight sleeper services were in decline, killed off by budget airlines and fast daytime TGV trains. He lovingly describes all the old routes, and his attempts to recreate for himself what is left of them today in spite of cancellations, being robbed, finding a stowaway in his compartment and having to put up with dreadful snack food. Still, he kept going, for the sheer love of travelling by train and an inner need to chronicle these iconic train routes before they vanish completely. He ends the book: 'This book has been written as a lament. But if it turns out that my tone is misconceived, and the European night trains will not disappear into a permanent darkness, I will be only too glad.' As one reviewer commented: 'No more the couchettes, the smell of steam, the all night bumping and clanging, the unexplained night stops in unknown provincial cities ...'.

However, lo and behold, since the book was published night sleeper trains have made something of a comeback, both in Britain and on the Continent. In Britain the Night Riviera service between London Paddington and Penzance has been refurbished with stylish interiors and a cocktail bar and the splendid Caledonian Sleeper which runs between London Euston and the Scottish Highlands has brand-new Mark 5 carriages with shower and en suite facilities in the cabins and a smart lounge car which serves appetising food and a wide range of drinks. You can even book a double bed with en suite facilities, sip your Highland malt whisky and eat haggis, neeps and tatties in the Club Car, as the train rolls through the wild Scottish scenery.

On the Continent disenchantment with short-haul flying combined with environmental concerns have made governments look again at overnight train travel. The French government has committed to reopening ten night services, starting with the Paris–Nice service, while Austria has invested heavily in its Nightjet trains, which are expected to reach Vienna, Budapest, Berlin, Milan, Rome and Zurich. And the European Sleeper now runs from Brussels in Belgium to Berlin in Germany, one of the oldest of the sleeper routes. You can now travel overnight from Hamburg to Stockholm in thirteen hours, from Stuttgart to Zagreb in sixteen hours, from Munich to Venice in eleven hours and Vienna to Bucharest in twenty hours, all in couchette, single or double berths. Slowly the romance of the night sleepers is returning, even if they can't match the glamour of the years between the world wars.

Moreover, as we have seen, with the returning popularity of overnight travel, writers of detective and mystery fiction have once again turned their attention to sleeper trains as the perfect setting for a gripping narrative. Just as a post-war generation of

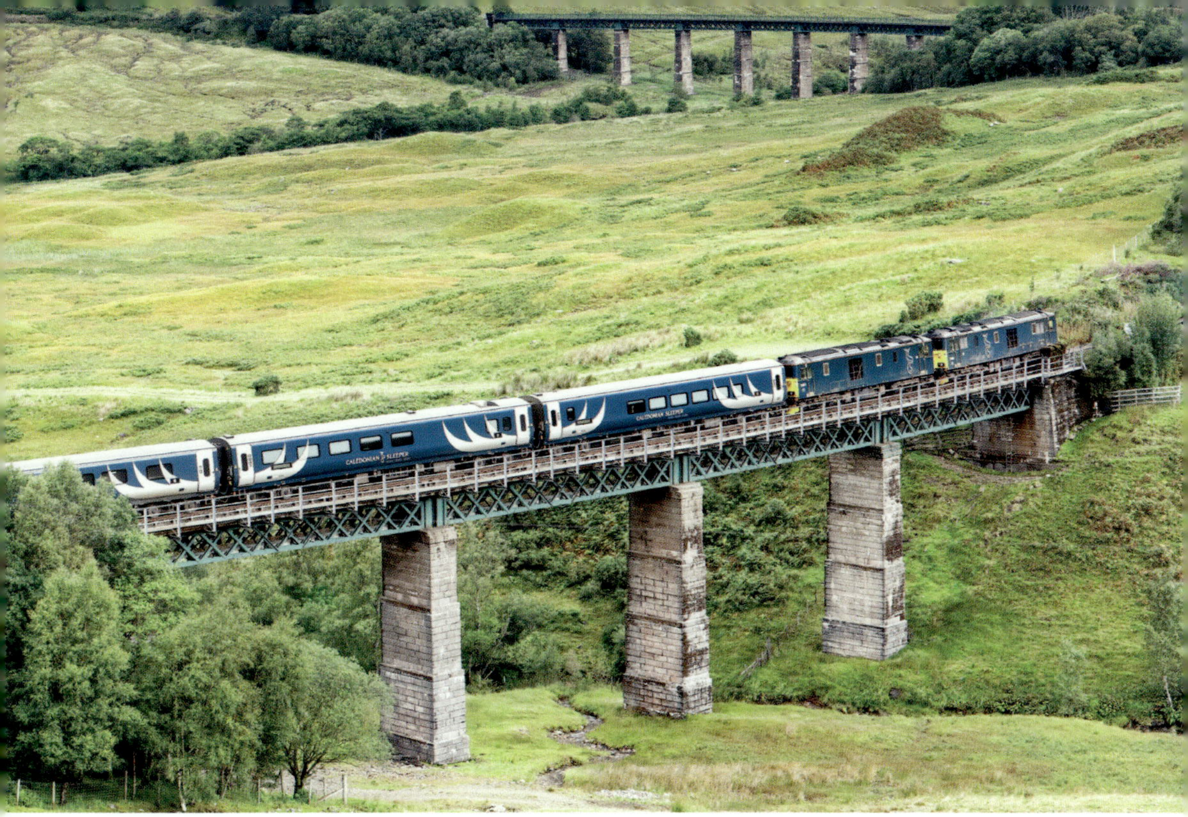

The Caledonian Sleeper with Mark 5 carriages crossing the Auch Viaduct, West Highland Line, Scotland. (Norman McNab)

novelists like Patricia Highsmith (*Strangers on a Train*, 1950), a psychological thriller in which two people who meet by chance on a train plot to 'trade' murders, and John Dickson Carr (*The Murder in Number Four*, 1981), a short story in which a murder takes place in a locked train compartment while several passengers think they see a ghost, have played with the setting of a train journey as the backdrop to a murder mystery, so more recent writers like the French author Sébastien Japrisot and the American mystery writer Stuart Kaminsky have used overnight trains, as in Japrisot's *The Sleeping Car Murders* (1962) and Kaminsky's *Murder on the Trans-Siberian Express* (2001). The children's author Michael Bond also ventured into the genre, with *Monsieur Pamplemousse Takes the Train* (1993), in which he takes the Rome-Paris Express, escorting his niece Caterina back to Paris, who promptly disappears when the train pulls into the Gare de Lyon.

British author C. J. Farrington has published three novels based around the Trans-Siberian Express, featuring his heroine Olga Pushkin, a railway engineer with a genius for detection, who lives in the village of Roslazny by the railway line. In his 2021 novel *Death on the Trans-Siberian Express* Olga is knocked unconscious by a man falling from the train, his throat cut and his mouth stuffed with 10 rouble coins. When the local policeman Sargeant Vassily Marushkin finds himself falsely imprisoned, Olga sets out to prove his innocence and solve the crime.

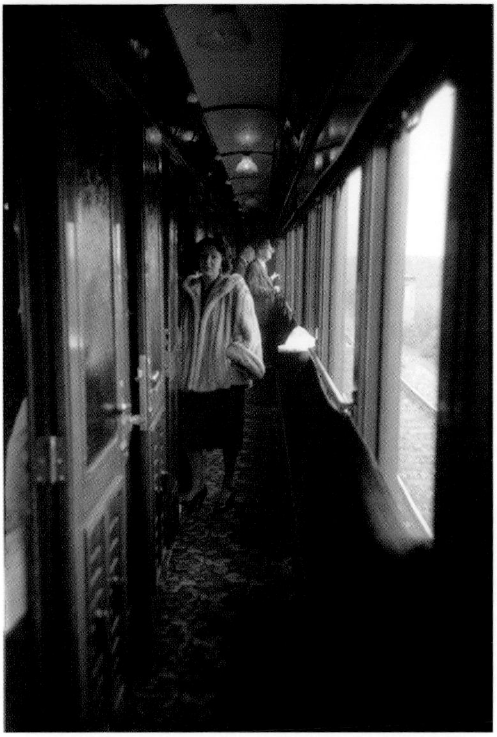

An unknown lady wearing a fur coat on the Simplon Orient Express, 1950. She told the photographer Jack Birns that she was a stateless Czech, and she had a German concentration camp number on her arm. The Madonna of the Sleeping Cars? (Shutterstock/*Life* Jack Birns)

Farrington, whose latest book *Last Stop on the Murder Express* was published in 2025, has said that as a fan of Agatha Christie he has always wanted to write a series of crime novels inspired by Christie's writing style: 'She could do more with fewer words than anyone else.'

Murder on the night sleeper is certainly back in business in the twenty-first century. You can even book a 'Murder Mystery' experience on one of the Belmond British Pullman trains, and on a number of preserved steam railways such as the Churnet Valley Railway or the East Lancashire Railway. I particularly liked the title of one evening event on the East Lancs: 'Murder on the Disorientated Express – A Hercule Poirot mystery of death!' We still love that sense of jeopardy, mystery and romance associated with night-time travel, people thrown together at random on a night train, who could be villains or heroes sleeping in the berth next to ours, or perhaps prowling the train plotting some dastardly deed. There could be trouble on the journey ahead ...

When used as the setting for murder, the sleeper train is sometimes incidental to the narrative, merely the starting point for an adventure that then takes place elsewhere (e.g. Josephine Tey's *The Singing Sands*), or the train is magnificently centre stage, an integral element in the unravelling of the mystery (e.g. Agatha Christie's *Murder on the Orient Express*). There are recurring devices which authors use, such as getting the train stuck in a snowdrift and the powerful sense of urgency and being propelled inexorably forward towards the train's destination, which help to heighten the dramatic tension and keep the plot moving along. Above all, many authors linger lovingly over the details of the trains, the carriages, the restaurant car, the engines and the rituals of departure and arrival.

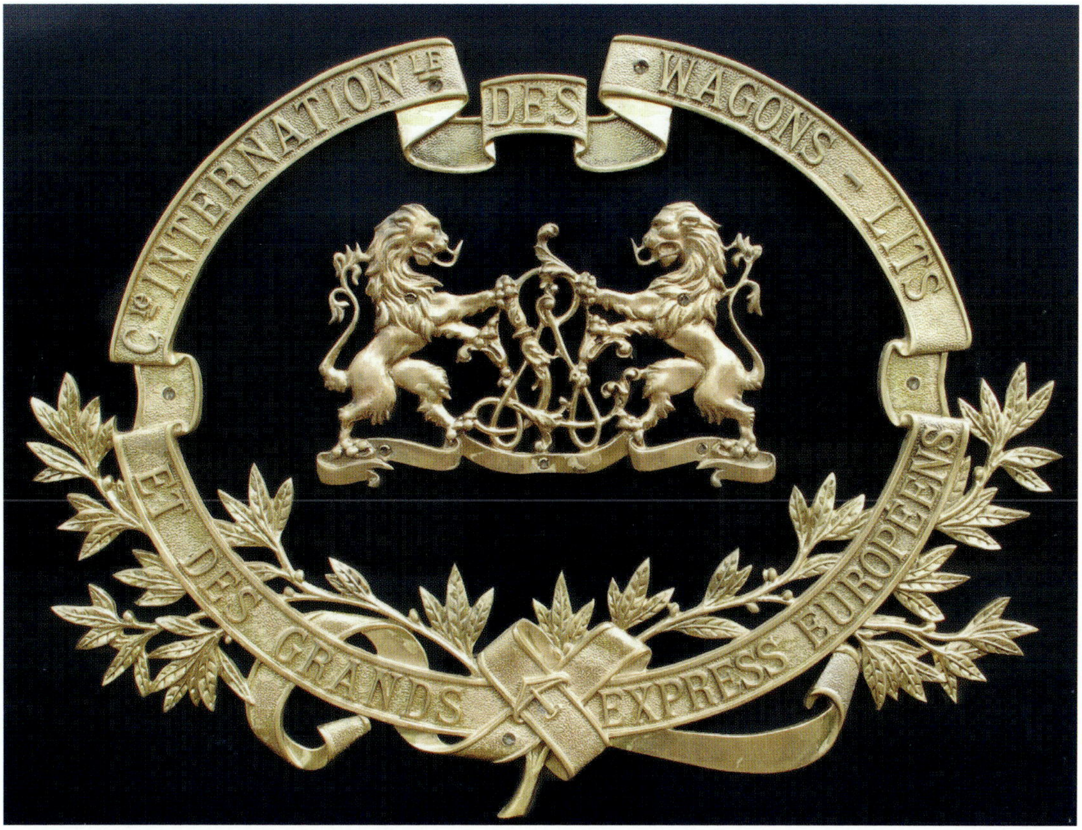

Logo of the Compagnie Internationale des Wagons-Lits. (CIWL archive (c Wagons-Lits Diffusion Phototeque))

We have seen how, over time, crime fiction has evolved from the genteel conventions of the Golden Age of Crime Fiction to the darker themes of modern psychological thrillers. In terms of style, the traditional 'whodunnit' structure has evolved into a more complex focus of shifting perspectives, more psychological depth and the avoidance of a neat resolution to the plot. Instead of detectives being celebrity characters, they have become more flawed and morally ambiguous. Instead of pure escapism, there is a greater willingness to tackle contemporary issues (Alexandra Benedict is a good example).

While the classic mystery thrillers of the past tend to be lighter in tone, more recent examples of the genre are often darker, and more intense, exploring deeper psychological issues. But whether classic, modern or somewhere in between, the novels we have been exploring all use the device of an overnight railway journey as the context for framing the narrative and generating the necessary tension and anxiety about what is going to happen next.

When travelling on a long-distance train, especially overnight, the passengers have to commit themselves to the flow of the train, propelled forward by the steam, diesel or electric locomotive. You don't have to be familiar with the history of that particular railway line to know that the engine driver and train crew are part of a long chain of people that stretches back to the original nineteenth-century track-layers, engineers and pioneers who established the route that is unfolding before you, a route that has a definite terminus and a published time of arrival. This sense of powerlessness, passivity and of jeopardy induced by the possibility of accident or delay has been harnessed very effectively by crime novelists who have written about trains. During the early years of railway travel doctors identified a condition called 'railway neurosis', a psychological affliction which began to be treated by the proponents of the emerging field of psychology. Gradually the human brain adjusted to the new phenomenon of railway travel and the neurosis subsided, but buried in our subconscious the old trauma remains, which unexpected interruptions or events in the course of a journey can trigger, heightened by the motion and confinement of the train. The order and predictability of a long train journey, running to a preordained timetable, can easily be disrupted by the disorder and unpredictability of the human personality when things go wrong. Graham Greene's *Stamboul Train* is a classic example. W. H. Auden, in his article about the detective story already mentioned, even goes as far as to propose a religious dimension to our enjoyment of murder/mystery fiction. He says that detective stories provide 'the magic formula' of an innocence which is discovered to contain guilt, which an outsider – the detective – takes away by pointing to the truly guilty person. 'The phantasy which the detective story addict indulges is the phantasy of being restored to the Garden of Eden, to a state of innocence.'

Whether Auden's analysis is true or not, there is no doubt that modern writers have used the genre to explore darker themes, our inner fears and anxieties, the sense of unease we feel when faced with wrongdoing and violence, and our feelings of relief and satisfaction when the uncertainties of the plot are resolved, the solution is revealed and normality is restored. In addition, in the murder mystery set on a sleeper train the tensions are heightened by the closed environment, the contrast between the comparative luxury and security of the train and the sense of jeopardy induced by the murder or robbery which

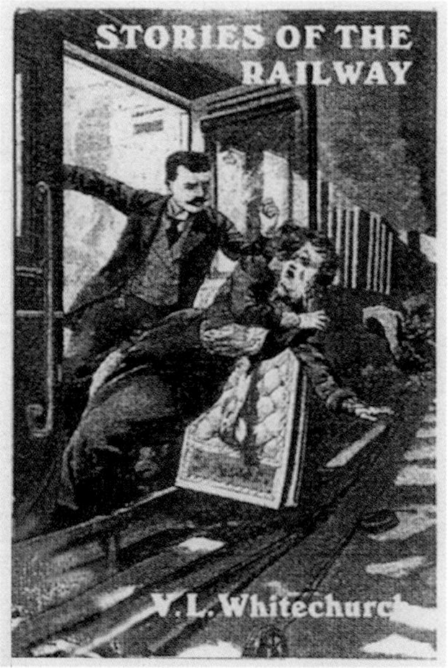

Book cover of Victor Whitechurch's *Thrilling Stories of the Railway*, 1912. (Author's collection)

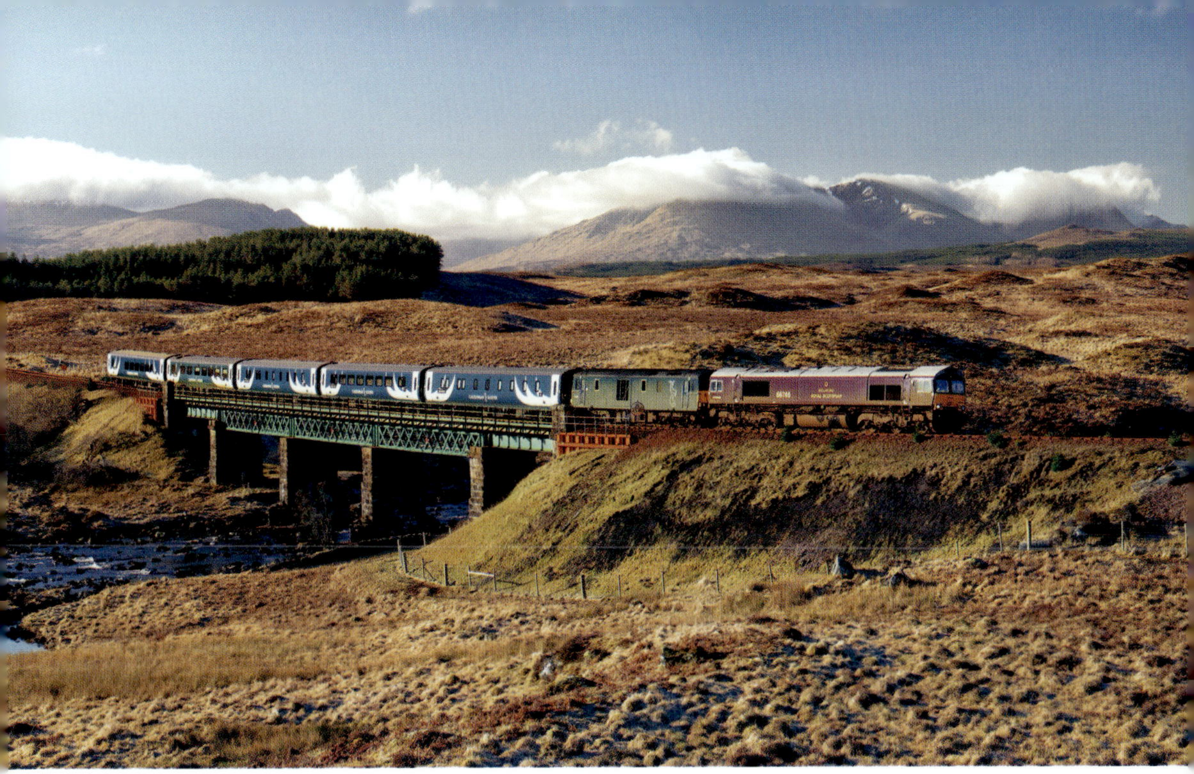

Northbound Caledonian Sleeper at Gaur Viaduct, 1 km south of Rannoch station, taken at 8.30 a.m. on 18 March 2025. (Norman McNab)

has taken place, and the onward propulsion of the train itself, surging forward towards its destination and heedless of the events which are disrupting its progress. All this suggests that the link between murder/mystery fiction and the railways will remain a strong and fruitful one in the years to come. Modern trains themselves may have become more homogeneous, bland and anonymous objects, with passengers sitting in isolation, buried in their laptops, iPads and smart phones, but the next wave of crime fiction could well harness all that as writers depict their characters' crimes as being masked by this deliberate avoidance of human contact – a murder, perhaps, hidden in plain sight while everyone is oblivious, absorbed in their headphones and mobile devices. After all, as Paul Theroux has said, 'Anything is possible on a train ...'.

Select Bibliography

This list does not pretend to be a comprehensive bibliography but includes works the author has found useful in writing this book, and others which involve sleeping cars or night trains in their narratives. I have also added a few films and a list of reference books about the history of railways which are pertinent to the theme.

Books

Eric Ambler	*The Mask of Dimitrios* (1939)
	Uncommon Danger (1937)
David Baldacci	*The Christmas Train* (2003)
Alexandra Benedict	*Murder on the Christmas Express* (2022)
Michael Bond	*Monsieur Pamplemousse Takes the Train* (1993)
John Buchan	*The Thirty-Nine Steps* (1915)
	Mr Standfast (1919)
Agatha Christie	*The Mystery of the Blue Train* (1928)
	Murder on the Orient Express (1934)
Manning Coles	*Night Train to Paris* (1952)
Freeman Wills Crofts	*Sir John Magill's Last Journey* (1930)
Maurice Dekobra	*The Madonna of the Sleeping Cars* (1927)
August Derleth	*The Adventure of the Orient Express* (1955)
Charles Dickens	*Dombey and Son* (1848)
	Mugby Junction (1866)
	The Signal Man (1866)
A. Den Doolaard	*Express to the East* (1936)
Arthur Conan Doyle	*The Adventures of Sherlock Holmes* (1892)
	The Memoirs of Sherlock Holmes (1894)
	The Return of Sherlock Holmes (1905)
	His Last Bow (1917)
	The Case-Book of Sherlock Holmes (1927)

C. J. Farrington	*Death on the Trans-Siberian Express* (2021)
	Last Stop on the Murder Express (2025)
Ian Fleming	*From Russia with Love* (1957)
Dick Francis	*The Edge* (1988)
Richard Austin Freeman	*When Rogues Fall Out* (1932)
Graham Greene	*Stamboul Train* (1932)
Arthur Griffiths	*The Passenger from Calais* (1906)
	The Rome Express (1907)
Paula Hawkins	*The Girl on the Train* (2015)
Patricia Highsmith	*Strangers on a Train* (1950)
Henry Holt	*The Midnight Mail* (1931)
Bohumil Hrabal	*Closely Watched Trains* (1965)
Dorothy Hughes	*Dread Journey* (1945)
Sébastien Japrisot	*The Sleeping Car Murders* (1962)
Stuart Kaminsky	*Murder on the Trans-Siberian Express* (2001)
M. G. Leonard and Sam Sedgman	*The Highland Falcon Thief* (2020)
Philip McCutchan	*Overnight Express* (1988)
Andrew Martin	*The Necropolis Railway* (2002)
Alfred Edward Woodley Mason	*The Summons* (1920)
Seichō Matsumoto	*Tokyo Express* (1958)
Hugh Morrison	*Death on the Night Train* (2022)
Vladimir Nabokov	*The Real Life of Sebastian Knight* (1941)
Frederick Nebel	*Sleepers East* (1933)
E. Nesbit	*The Railway Children* (1905)
Anthony Parsons	*The Mystery of the Cairo Express* (1944)
Austin Phillips	*The Man on the Night Mail* (1927)
John Rhode	*Death on the Boat Train* (1940)
Cecil Roberts	*Victoria, Four-Thirty* (1937)
Mary Roberts Rinehart	*The Man in Lower Ten* (1909)
Georges Simenon	*My Friend Maigret* (1949)
Josephine Tey	*The Singing Sands* (1952)
Ethel Lina White	*The Wheel Spins* (1936)
Emile Zola	*La Bête humaine* (1890)

Short Stories

John Dickson Carr	*The Murder in Number Four* (reprinted in John Dickson Carr, *The Door to Doom and Other Detections* (1981))
Freeman Wills Crofts	*The 9.50 Up Express and Other Stories* (2020) (includes full biography and bibliography)
	The Mystery of the Sleeping Car Express (1921)
Martin Edwards (ed.)	*Blood on the Tracks: Railway Mysteries* (2018)
William McGivern	*The Sound of Murder* (1952)

G. Radcliffe	*On the Irish Mail* (in Dorothy Sayers, *Great Short Stories of Detection, Mystery and Horror*, 3rd Series (1934)
Bill Pronzini	*Midnight Specials* (1977)
Robert Louis Stevenson	*The Rajah's Diamond* (1878)
Thomas Walsh	*Journey by Night* (1951)
Edith Wharton	*A Journey* (1890s)
Victor Whitechurch	*Thrilling Stories of the Railway* (1912)
	The Thorpe Hazell Mysteries: And More Thrilling Tales On and Off the Rails (2010)

Films

Broccoli/Saltzman	*From Russia with Love* (1963)
Eugene Forde	*Sleepers West* (1941)
Alfred Hitchcock	*The Lady Vanishes* (1938)
Richard Irving	*Istanbul Express* (1968)
Joseph von Sternberg	*Shanghai Express* (1932)
Billy Wilder	*Some Like It Hot* (1959)

TV Series

Nick Leather	*Nightsleeper* (2024)

Non-Fiction

Michael Barsley	*Orient Express* (1966)
George Behrend	*The History of Wagons-Lits* (1959)
	Grand European Expresses (1962)
	History of Trains de Luxe (1972)
	Night Ferry (1985)
Simon Bradley	*The Railways* (2015)
E. H. Cookridge	*Orient Express* (1978)
Garry Hogg	*Orient Express* (1968)
K. W. Jones	*Romantic Railways* (1971)
Andrew Martin	*Night Trains* (2017)
David Meara	*Anglo-Scottish Sleepers* (2018)
Philip L. Scowcroft	*Railways in British Crime Fiction* (CADS No. 9 2004)
Shirley Sherwood	*The Venice Simplon Orient Express* (1983)
Paul Theroux	*The Great Railway Bazaar* (1975)